chAg
ALL

Marc Chagall

James Johnson Sweeney

Marc Chagall

In collaboration with The Art Institute of Chicago

THE MUSEUM OF MODERN ART, NEW YORK

Contents

	Page
Acknowledgments	4
Chronology	5
Photograph of the artist by Lotte Jacobi	6
Marc Chagall by James Johnson Sweeney	7
The Prints of Marc Chagall by Carl O. Schniewind	72
Catalog of the Exhibition	87
One-man Exhibitions	90
Works by Chagall in American Public Collections	91
Illustrated Books	92
Theatre Designs	92
Bibliography by Hannah B. Muller	93

Color Plates:

I and the Village	19
The Praying Jew	35
Time is a River without Banks	65

The drawings for the end leaves and title page were made by the artist especially for this catalog.

ACKNOWLEDGMENTS

In addition to those who have lent to the exhibition I wish to thank the following for their co-operation: Mrs. Lisa Arnhold, Miss Elmira Bier, Emil E. Bendix, Mrs. Louis Bergman, Jean Bernheim, Henry Bernheim, Mme Lia Bernstein, Galerie de Berri, Mr. and Mrs. Albert Blum, Mrs. Adelyn D. Breeskin, Mme Jeanne Bucher, Miss Doris Budrow, Frederick Mortimer Clapp, Miss Louisa Dresser, H. G. Dwight, Paul Farish, René Gaffé, Paul Ganz, Robert Giron, Miss Verna Harrison, Arthur Holde, Gerard Hordijk, Robin Ironside, George Jacoubovsky, H. W. Janson, Miss Una E. Johnson, Marcel Kapferer, Karl Kup, Baroness Lambert, Dr. Bartholomew Landheer, Charles Leirens, Prof. Claude Lévi-Strauss, The Board of Burgomasters and Aldermen of the City of Liège, Belgium, Mrs. Robert Magidoff, Miss Ruth S. Magurn, Mr. and Mrs. Burgess Meredith, Prof. S. Michoels, Miss Natalie Munson, Gerald Murphy, J. B. Neumann, Karl Nierendorf, Jacques Ochs, Mlle Claire Pels, Maurice Potin, Michel Rapaport, Ernest Rathenau, Perry T. Rathbone, Baroness Hilla von Rebay, Mrs. Mary Reynolds, W. J. H. B. Sandberg, Mrs. Daniel Saidenberg, Frederick B. Serger, Henri A. Seyrig, Miss Catherine Viviano, Miss Mary Katherine Woodworth, Christian Zervos.

Particular acknowledgment for their help in research and in the assembling of the exhibition is due to: H. W. L. Dana, Marcel Duchamp, Jan-Albert Goris, Louis Lozowick, Mr. and Mrs. Pierre Matisse, Mrs. Marjorie D. Mathias, Daniel Catton Rich, Carl O. Schniewind, Frau Nell Urech-Walden, Hans van Weeren-Griek, Miss Nika Pleshkova of the Museum Staff.

And I am especially indebted to the artist and his daughter, Ida Gordey, for their patient courtesy and assistance throughout the preparations for the exhibition; to Mr. John Dos Passos for his generosity in translating Blaise Cendrars' poem on Chagall; to Miss Margaret Miller for the painstaking care she has given to the preparation of the catalog, for her invaluable suggestions and revisions of the text, and for her important part in the installation; to Miss Frances Pernas for her assistance in seeing the catalog through the press; and to Carlus Dyer for the design of the cover and format of this book.

LENDERS

Mr. and Mrs. Walter C. Arensberg, Hollywood; Mlle Marcelle Berr de Turique, Neuilly-sur-Seine, France; Mr. and Mrs. Joseph Bissett, New York; Marc Chagall, New York; Philippe Dotremont, Uccle-Brussels, Belgium; Hjalmar Gabrielson, Gothenburg, Sweden; Mrs. Charles B. Goodspeed; Miss Ida Gordey; Baron Edward von der Heydt, Ascona, Switzerland; Miss Mary E. Johnston, Glendale, Ohio; Adolphe A. Juviler, New York; John S. Newberry, Jr., Grosse Pointe Farms, Michigan; The Vicomte de Noailles, Paris, France; Mr. and Mrs. Walter Paepcke, Chicago; Dr. Potvin, Brussels, Belgium; P. A. Regnault, Laren, Holland; Mme Helena Rubinstein, New York; Louis E. Stern, New York; Josef von Sternberg, Hollywood; Frau Nell Urech-Walden, Schinznach-Bad, Aargau, Switzerland.

The Art Institute of Chicago, Chicago; City Art Museum of St. Louis, St. Louis; Municipal Museum, Amsterdam, Holland; Museum of Fine Arts, Liège, Belgium; The Museum of Modern Art, New York; The Solomon R. Guggenheim Foundation, New York; The Worcester Museum, Worcester, Mass.

Pierre Matisse Gallery, New York.

CHRONOLOGY

1889 Born Vitebsk, Russia, July 7.

1907 Began painting; Pen Academy, Vitebsk. Moved to St. Petersburg.

1907–1910 St. Petersburg. Entered Imperial School for the Protection of the Fine Arts; later studied with Leon Bakst.

1910–1914 To Paris. Exhibited at the *Salon des Indépendants*. Met Blaise Cendrars, Canudo, Guillaume Apollinaire.

1914–1915 March, to Berlin; exhibition at galleries of *Der Sturm:* later to Vitebsk, Russia. Married, 1915. Mobilized into army.

1915–1917 Petrograd; October Revolution, 1917; returned to Vitebsk.

1917–1919 Vitebsk. Appointed Minister of Arts for Vitebsk, 1918; directed art academy. First monograph on the artist (Efross and Tugendhold) published in Moscow.

1919–1922 Moscow. Executed murals for Granovsky's *Jewish State Theatre*. Wrote autobiography.

1922 Left Russia for Berlin; first etchings, *Mein Leben,* series, commissioned by Paul Cassirer.

1923 Invited to Paris by Vollard. Began illustrations for Gogol's *Dead Souls*.

1924 First retrospective exhibition, *Galerie Barbazanges-Hodebert*.

1925–1926 Gouaches and etchings to illustrate the *Fables* of La Fontaine.

1926 First New York one-man show, Reinhardt Galleries.

1930 Autobiography, *Ma Vie,* published in France. Began illustration of Bible.

1933 Large retrospective exhibition, Basel.

1931–1937 Trips to Egypt, Syria, Palestine, 1931; Holland, 1932; Spain, 1934; Poland, 1935; Italy, 1937.

1939 World War II; moved to Gordes, France.

1941 To U.S.A.

1942 Mexico (3 months). Scenery and costume designs for ballet, *Aleko*.

1944 Death of Bella Chagall.

1945 Scenery and costume designs for *Firebird*.

Photograph by Lotte Jacobi

Marc Chagall

Marc Chagall

"It is the glory and the misery of the artist's lot" as André Lhôte once said, "to transmit a message of which he does not possess the translation."* This is particularly applicable to Marc Chagall.

When Chagall first arrived in Paris in 1910, cubism held the center of the stage. French art was still dominated by the materialist outlook of the 19th century. Fifty years earlier naturalism and realism had opened the way to impressionism. Impressionism's analyses of light on objects had led to cubism's analyses of the objects themselves. Little by little the manner of representing an object had come to have a greater interest than the subject—the physical character of the painting more importance than its power to awake associational responses in the observer. Chagall arrived from the East with a ripe color gift, a fresh, unashamed response to sentiment, a feeling for simple poetry and a sense of humor. He brought with him a notion of painting quite foreign to that esteemed at the time in Paris. His first recognition there came not from painters, but from poets such as Blaise Cendrars and Guillaume Apollinaire. To him the cubists' conception seemed "earthbound." He felt it was "necessary to change nature not only materially and from the outside, but also from within, ideologically, without fear of what is known as 'literature.' "† And his approach to a certain degree anticipated that reaction from the materialist, or physical emphasis in painting which was to announce itself two or three years later in the work of Marcel Duchamp and to flower in the surrealist movement of the nineteen-twenties.

Unlike so many of the vanguard artists in Paris at that time, Chagall employed readily recognizable representational forms in his work. Still if you ask Chagall to explain his paintings even today he will reply: "I don't understand them at all. They are not literature. They are only pictorial arrangements of images that obsess me . . . The theories which I would make up to explain myself and those which others elaborate in connection with my work are nonsense . . . My paintings are my reason for existence, my life and that's all."

Yet it was with Marc Chagall in his early Paris work, as André Breton has said, "and with him alone, that the metaphor made its triumphant return into modern painting."‡ This is Chagall's contribution to contemporary art: the reawakening of a poetry of representation, avoiding factual illustration on the one hand, and non-figurative abstractions on the other.

* Bibl. 102. † Raynal, bibl. 143. ‡ Bibl. 35, page 89.

EARLY YEARS: A SOURCE OF RECOLLECTIONS

Marc Chagall was born in Vitebsk, Russia on July 7, 1889. Vitebsk, at the time of Chagall's birth, was a city of some 60,000 inhabitants. It is an old town—mentioned by the Byzantine chroniclers as early as the 10th century—situated on both banks of the river Dwina about eighty miles northwest of Smolensk. In Chagall's boyhood it was a typical provincial capital, with its pear-domed church towers, its stone buildings painted a striking yellow, its modest gray wooden buildings, its interminable wooden fences and its packed Jewish quarter. More than half its population were Jews. This was the town in which Chagall's early years were passed and which, in recollection, was to provide him with the subject matter for so many of his pictures. This was the "sad and joyful city," as he calls it, of his youth.

His father worked in a herring depot. The family was a large one: he had eight sisters and a brother. The atmosphere in which he was brought up was deeply religious. Day after day, he recalls, winter as well as summer, his father arose at six o'clock in the morning and went to the synagogue. Prayer and ritual color all his earlier memories, as fasts and feasts date them—Pasch, Sukkot, Simhat Torah. His paternal grandfather was a religious instructor, and his mother's father, a butcher in Lyozno, spent half his day in the synagogue. His Uncle Neuch, who also lived in Lyozno, had a violin. He was an ardent Chasidist. Every evening after his long day in the butcher shop he would play the rabbi's song; every Saturday he would put on a thalis, or prayer shawl, and read the Bible aloud.

There were, as he puts it, "half-a-dozen uncles or a little more." And he had as many aunts, each of whom likewise made her contribution to the family folklore which was to supply the elements of so much of his work in later years. For, as he says, "if my art did not play any role in the life of my relatives, on the other hand their life and their creations have greatly influenced me . . . It doesn't matter to me if people discover with joy and satisfaction the enigma of my paintings in these innocent adventures of my relatives." *

* Unless otherwise noted, all subsequent quotations from Chagall are taken from his autobiography (bibl. 5), written about 1920.

Candles in the Dark Street of 1908 (below), so often described as his "first illogical or fantastic painting" is a good example of the manner in which he turns such material into "fantasy" by those curious representational juxtapositions which we have come to associate with his work.

In his autobiography he recounts an anecdote of his Lyozno grandfather. In the course of festivities, one Sukkot, or Simhat Torah, his grandfather was found to be missing. They searched on all sides for him. Finally, it was discovered that his grandfather had climbed to the roof because the weather was so good and was sitting there quietly regaling himself on raw carrots.

When we add to this story the phrase he employs of his Uncle Neuch's musicianship "He played the violin like a shoemaker," we recognize in these combined recollections the iconographic source of both the fiddler seated on the rooftop and the shoemaker's shop sign in the upper left-hand corner of the picture.

Then if we turn to another recollection in his autobiography, that of his first encounter with death, we find the rest of the subject matter of the picture: "One morning before dawn suddenly I heard cries from the street below my windows. By the feeble glimmer of the night lamp I managed to distinguish a woman running alone down the deserted street. She waved her arms, sobbed, begged the neighbors who were still asleep to come to save her husband as if I,

Candles in the Dark Street (La Mort). 1908. Oil, 26¾ x 34″. Owned by the artist.

Portrait of My Fiancée in Black Gloves. 1909. Oil, 34¾ x 25¼″. Collection Baron Edward von der Heydt, Ascona, Switzerland.

or my fat cousin sound asleep in her bed, could cure or save a dying man." A few paragraphs further on: "The dead man, solemnly sad, is already stretched out on the ground, his face lighted by six candles. In the end they carry him away. Our street is no longer the same. I do not recognize it."

But in depicting it Chagall has heaped up his various recollections—even to its most familiar figure, the street sweeper—and out of these disparate elements he has made his picture. It is not an anecdote, not even a correlation of details. There is a certain amount of naturalism in the constituent elements if they are taken individually. But visual perspective is in the main disregarded in favor of a perspective of values common to mediaeval and primitive art, the more important features being given the greater size. And this apparently illogical grouping of naturalistic features is the basis of the painting's metaphorical character—a resemblance to a group of literary images with suppressed connectives.

BEGINNINGS

At the age of thirteen Chagall began, as he says, "to know the intoxication of drawing." His home environment and the iconoclasm of his religion's tradition gave his enthusiasm little encouragement. It was hoped he might make the place for himself in the tradesman's world of Vitebsk which his father failed to do. He continued his school work unhappily and unremuneratively another four years. Then, one day, he announced that he had decided to give it all up to become a painter. He had heard of an "academy," directed by a painter named Pen, Vitebsk's only art school, and he had set his heart on attending it.

With his mother's aid he was enrolled. He remained there scarcely three months. Nevertheless, it was a beginning.

St. Petersburg was the next step. Meanwhile he had been apprenticed to a photographer. But he detested the work of retouching photographs. A bourgeois fellow-student from Pen's, with whom he painted in the country on weekends, suggested the capital; and Chagall prevailed on his father to let him go.

But to live in St. Petersburg under the Czar a Jew had also to have a special authorization. Through a shop-keeper friend his father arranged a temporary certificate which permitted the boy to enter the city for the ostensible purpose of accepting the delivery of some merchandise.* His friend was to follow shortly afterwards. And Chagall, with twenty-seven rubles in his pocket —all that his father could give him—set out, at the age of seventeen, for his new life, alone.

ST. PETERSBURG 1907-1909

As soon as possible after his arrival in St. Petersburg he took the entrance examinations for Baron Stieglitz' School of Arts and Crafts. He failed. Something had to be found at once to give him the legal right to remain in the capital. He turned to a third class school—the School of the Society for the Protection of the Arts—and there won a year's scholarship with an allowance of ten rubles a month. Following this, one or two patrons aided him for brief periods. He shared lodgings with laborers; he worked as a domestic servant in a lawyer's home. But his Jewish status gave him more trouble than his financial straits. Finally, after a stay in jail for lack of working papers, he decided he had to learn a trade. He apprenticed himself to a sign painter in order to obtain a certificate from a professional school. The prospect of an examination worried him. He knew he "could paint fruit or a Turk smoking," but he was sure he would fail the lettering test. Nevertheless signs interested him—he had always wanted to paint them—and he went to work industriously at this new occupation and produced a whole series.

At the same time he continued to attend the School for the Protection of Fine Arts. But finally he came to realize the futility of it. The two years he had spent seemed wasted. The school

* To obtain a permit to go his father had to advance Chagall's age two years. As a result the year of his birth has regularly been given as 1887 instead of 1889.

My Studio. Paris, 1910. Oil, 23¾ x 28¾". Owned by the artist.

of Bakst had just then begun to attract attention. It was the only school in St. Petersburg with a breath of Western Europe blowing through it. Bakst was a member of the *Mir Iskusstva*, or World of Art group which had grown out of the periodical of the same name, founded by Diaghileff in 1899. This group included such artists as Benois, Golovin, Somov, Roerich, Serov and others, and was essentially an "art for art's sake" movement. It had originated as a reaction from the academy with the aim of welcoming new influences into Russia. But it admitted so many different trends—the only apparent requisite being novelty—that it had degenerated into a modish, stylizing eclecticism. Chagall was soon to realize this. Yet after two fruitless years at the School for the Protection of Arts the possibility of joining a class where fresh ideas were even discussed, much less welcomed, was in itself exhilarating to Chagall. He had to enroll—even though the fee was thirty rubles a month.

He presented himself timorously to Bakst. Bakst accepted him. At the next easel was the dancer, Nijinsky, and in the same class was the Countess Tolstoy. But Chagall soon saw that Bakst's teaching was not for him. Within three months he was back again in Vitebsk.

RETURN TO VITEBSK 1909

Still if he had learned nothing from his teachers in St. Petersburg they had done him no harm. And shortly after his return to Vitebsk he was producing those first canvases in which today we recognize the promise of the mature artist: *Birth*, with its naive attention to realistic details, *Candles in the Dark Street* (page 9), *Portrait of My Fiancée in Black Gloves* (page 10), and *The Wedding* (page 15). From these it is evident that he would not have been able to accept the polite, emasculate approach of Bakst, or to fit in with the *Mir Iskusstva* group. Here was a realist, a genre painter, steeped in the color of his tiny provincial world. Even in these paintings the somber, sullen tones seem to suggest the sad pleasures and constantly impending tragedy of the Jewish quarter in which he had grown up. Here he is the intuitive expressionist—making use of chiaroscuro to externalize his emotions, and distortions to underscore the lyrical or pathetic aspects of his subjects: birth, death, marriage—with *The Wedding* scarcely gayer than *Candles in the Dark Street*.

Then once again came the urge to move on. It was Paris now. In St. Petersburg he had at least learned that Paris was the center of the world he dreamt of. He was tired of the provinces—

"Vitebsk, I am leaving you.
Stay alone with your herrings."

But first it was necessary to return to St. Petersburg. On his arrival there he had the good fortune to be presented to a celebrated attorney named Vinaver, a member of the Duma, and leader of the Constitutionalist Democratic party. Vinaver admired Chagall, and Chagall in turn came to regard him almost as another father. As he says "my father put me into the world, Vinaver made a painter of me. Without him I would probably have remained a photographer in Vitebsk without any idea of Paris."

Vinaver put him up near his own home in the offices of the review, *Razviet*. He bought the first two paintings Chagall ever sold—one the 1909 *Wedding*—and was untiring in his encouragement of the young artist. Finally, towards the end of 1910, he gave Chagall a monthly allowance which would permit him to live in Paris and sent him on his way.

PARIS

Four days on a train across Europe—Paris—and Chagall confesses that only the great distance that separated him from his native city kept him from returning at once, or at least within a week or month after his arrival.

It was the Louvre, the salons and the galleries of the Rue Lafitte and the Place de la Madeleine that held him: Manet, Delacroix, Courbet, van Gogh, Gauguin, Matisse and Bonnard; Renoir, Pissarro, Monet; Chardin, Fouquet, Géricault. The day after his arrival he went to the Salon des Indépendants. "I penetrated" as he says, "to the heart of French painting of 1910. I hooked myself there."

As soon as he found his way about, he gave up his studio in the Impasse du Maine for one more suited to his means in La Ruche. This was a curious beehive-like structure in a garden near the Abattoirs de Vaugirard built by the sculptor Boucher, a descendant of the 18th century painter of the same name, from lumber salvaged from the demolition of one of the Paris expositions. It comprised about two dozen wedge-shape studios, twelve on the ground floor for sculptors, twelve for painters on the floor above. Modigliani had the studio next to Chagall's; Léger, Soutine, and others on the same landing.

He soon made the acquaintance of the poet, Blaise Cendrars. The poet, Rubiner, was a frequent companion. And Canudo, the editor of *Montjoie*, became even embarrassing in his intemperate championing of the young painter's work. Chagall tells the story of a note of introduction Canudo urged him to take round to present to the collector, Jacques Doucet, with a packet of watercolors. After a quarter of an hour Doucet's valet returned with the message from his master, "We have no need of the best colorist of our day!"

Max Jacob, André Salmon and Delaunay, whose canvases in the salon always struck him by their dimensions, were his friends. And every Friday at Canudo's he would meet Gleizes, Metzinger, La Fresnaye, Léger, Segonzac, Lhôte, Luc-Albert Moreau, and others.

Yet that nostalgia which he had felt so deeply on his arrival in Paris was to set the tone and provide the inspiration for all his work of the period, steadily evolving though it was. Like that other precursor of surrealism, Giorgio de Chirico, who, unknown to Chagall, was painting his nostalgic recollections of Italian architecture in Paris at the same time, Chagall rarely lost sight of the Vitebsk of his boyhood, even though the yellow houses, the "white voluminous church at the center of the large square" and the interminable wooden fences might at times become chaotically scrambled in his pictures with the Eiffel Tower and the Champ de Mars.

RECOLLECTIONS

In his earliest Paris work such as *My Studio*, 1910 (page 12), Chagall is still the native expressionist—warmer and brighter in color than in his Vitebsk work—a Soutine, as it were, before Soutine. Even here we have the reminder of the early days in his *Portrait of My Fiancée in Black Gloves* on the studio wall; and in *The Wedding* of 1910 (page 16) we see him plunging back into home-town memories. But if we compare it with the 1909 wedding picture which he left in St. Petersburg with Vinaver, we see how profoundly his pictorial approach has changed, even though the subject matter is practically the same. There is an increased emphasis on the flat character of the picture surface in the 1910 painting in contrast to the receding perspective of the earlier

The Wedding. 1909. Oil. Formerly Vinaver Collection, Paris.

version. The beginnings of this were already visible in his Vitebsk *Burial*,* painted before his departure for Paris. In the 1910 painting the converging lines in the center foreground are used to focus attention on the bride and her father. This triangle is carefully kept clear so that the most important protagonists remain in the open and are not lost in the wedding procession. Towards the same end—and also to stress the plane surface of the canvas—the wedding procession is made to walk across the picture rather than to thread its way down out of the picture's depth. The influence of cubism is possibly recognizable in the sharp angles and the mixed perspective treatment of the houses. In short, we recognize here a development in the structural organization of the canvas and in the composition of individual elements which has already moved quite a distance from the naturalistic space box of *The Wedding* or *Candles in the Dark Street.*

I and the Village (opposite page 18) of the next year carries all these trends quite a step further. Here cubism's respect for the plane of canvas is even more clearly illustrated. The composition of the rectangle is still tighter than in *The Wedding* through a greater disregard for a naturalistic treatment of space. And this picture offers an ideal exemplification of Chagall's statement: "I fill up the empty space in my canvas as the structure of my picture requires with a body or an object according to my humor." The composite strikes one first, then the details: first the large profiles, then smaller reminders of life in Vitebsk: the milkmaid, the farmer and his companion and the neighborhood church. Chagall, like the expressionists, uses color and line to underscore emotion, but also makes the details serve as emotional comments, footnotes or glosses.

* Reproduced in Venturi, bibl. 181, pl. 1.

The Wedding. Paris, 1910. Oil, 39⅛ x 74¼″. Owned by the artist.

The same holds for *Dedicated to My Fiancée* (page 21). While the mood of *I and the Village* is idyllic, and this quality is supported by the delicate tonalities and gentle rhythms, *Dedicated to My Fiancée* is a passionate expression in bold vermilions, greens and golds organized in violent rhythms. It is easily comprehensible that the force of this picture's colors and the turbulence of its rhythms should have reinforced the pornographic interpretation which led the censors of the Salon des Indépendants to request its withdrawal. Chagall and a companion protested that there was absolutely nothing pornographic about it. After some consideration the authorities allowed it to remain.

POETRY

The poet Blaise Cendrars was possibly Chagall's closest friend in these days. He admired Chagall's approach in painting, perhaps because of its basic similarity to his own in poetry. For him the verbal image was "a double-faced image" which on the one side "looks into the depths of the mind and on the other is reflected in the creative mechanism of sound. Considered in its material realization, it is translated by sounds, but through its psychic origins it is the product of the labor of the spirit . . . the verbal image is a psychic unity anterior to the word."* For him Rimbaud's *Enfance* was a poem of "pure psychic unity." Its contrast of individual images and their untranslatable fusion in the whole offers a striking comparison with what Chagall achieves in his most characteristic paintings:

* Blaise Cendrars, *Aujourd'hui*, Paris, 1931, p. 201.

Half-Past Three (The Poet). 1911. Oil, 78 x 57″. Collection Mr. and Mrs. Walter C. Arensberg, Hollywood.

Au bois il y a un oiseau, son chant vous arrête et vous fait rougir.

Il y a une horloge qui ne sonne pas.

Il y a une fondrière avec un nid de bêtes blanches.

Il y a une cathédrale qui descend et un lac qui monte.

Il y a une petite voiture abandonnée dans le taillis ou qui descend le sentier en courant, enrubannée.

Il y a une troupe de petits comédiens en costumes, aperçus sur la route à travers la lisière du bois.

Il y a enfin, quand l'on a faim et soif, quelqu'un qui vous chasse.

Translation on page 102.

While Chagall had a deep respect for the craftsmanship of painting and felt that in Paris those days one imbibed it almost without effort, he looked deeper for the real sense of art. He felt that French painting, from the neo-classicism of David and Ingres to the disciples of Cézanne and the cubists, had been interesting itself in surface features, and that even his leading Paris contemporaries were afraid to plunge into the chaos—"to break the accustomed surface and turn it upside down under their feet." He "personally did not feel that the scientific trend was beneficial to art. Impressionism and cubism," he said, "are alien to me . . . Art seems to be above all a state of the soul."

This was probably the ground on which his poet friends found his work so congenial, just as the surrealist poets were later to find Giorgio de Chirico's. André Breton is reputed to have given Chirico's paintings some of his most enigmatic titles. And Chagall tells us that Cendrars contributed many to his: *St. Voiturier*, *Half-Past Three* (page 17), and *To Russia, Asses and Others* (page 25), with its mild, avowedly anti-Czarist note more evident in Cendrars' title than in the actual content of the picture. In return it has been said that Chagall's painting played an important part in the inspiration of Cendrars' *Prose du Transsibérien.* And one of the most successful of his *Dix-Neuf Poèmes Elastiques* is the two-part poem—a portrait of Chagall and a description of his studio in La Ruche:

I. PORTRAIT

He's asleep
He's awake.
Right away he's painting
He grabs a church and paints with the church
He grabs a cow and paints with the cow
With a sardine
With heads, hands, knives

I and the Village. 1911. Oil on canvas, 75⅝ x 59⅝″. The Museum of Modern Art, Mrs. Simon Guggenheim Fund.

Dedicated to My Fiancée. 1911. Oil, 77 x 45¼″. Owned by the artist.

The Soldier Drinks. 1912. Oil, 43 x 37⅛″. Collection Frau Nell Urech-Walden, Schinznach-Bad, Switzerland.

He paints with an oxtail
With all the dirty passions of a little Jewish town
With all the exacerbated sexuality of provincial Russia
For France
Without sensuality
He paints with his hips
He has eyes in his hinder parts
Suddenly it's your portrait
It's you gentle reader
It's me
It's him
It's his betrothed
It's the corner grocer
The girl who brings home the cows
The midwife

There are puddles of blood
They are washing newborn babies in them
Skies gone mad
The latest thing in mouths
The corkscrew Tower
Hands
Christ
He's Christ himself
He passed his childhood on the cross
He cuts his own throat every day
Suddenly he's not painting any more
He was awake
But now he's asleep
He's choking on his cravat
Chagall is astonished to be still alive.

Homage to Apollinaire, Cendrars, Canudo and Walden. 1911-12. Oil.
Lange Collection, Krefeld, Germany.

II. STUDIO

La Ruche

Stairways doors stairways
And his door opens like a newspaper
Covered with visiting cards
And then it closes again.
Disorder, this is the land of disorder
There are photographs of Léger, photographs of Tobeen that you really don't see
And behind your back
Behind your back
Frenetic works
Sketches designs frenetic works
And oil paintings . . .
"We guarantee the absolute purity of our
Catsup"
Says a label
The window is an almanach
When the giant steamshovels of the lightning raucously unload the barges of the sky and empty the rumbling dumpcarts of thunder
The heavens fall
Pellmell

Cossacks the Christ a rotting sun
Roofs
Sleepwalkers a few goats
A werewolf
Petrus Borel
Insanity winter
A genii split like a peach
Lautréamont
Chagall
Poor child beside my wife
Morose enjoyment
His shoes are down at the heels
There's an old stewpan full of chocolate
You see the lamp double
And my drunkenness when I go to see him
Empty bottles
Bottles
Zina
(*We talked of her*)
Chagall
Chagall
Astride ladders of light

Translated by John Dos Passos.

To Russia, Asses and Others. 1911. Oil, 61⅝ x 48⅛″. Pierre Matisse Gallery, New York.

CUBISM

Cendrars was an intimate of Fernand Léger and a close friend of all the cubists. And while Chagall may have felt a materialist superficiality in their researches, he did not refuse to learn from them. In his painting *To Russia, Asses and Others* (above) he had already begun to break up naturalistic forms to adapt them to his compositional needs—"to fill empty spaces," as he put it. In *The Drunkard* this procedure is carried a step further and the decapitated head and flying bottle are used to create a focal center for his composition. A comparison of these pictures from another viewpoint shows clearly Chagall's sustained interest in the cubist's emphasis on the composition of the plane of the canvas over the pictorial illusion of space—just as we saw it

The Cattle Dealer. 1912. Oil, 38⅛ x 78⅞". Collection Frau Nell Urech-Walden, Schinznach-Bad, Switzerland.

in the comparison of his two earlier wedding paintings. Finally in *Half-Past Three* (page 17) he employs a full cubist freedom in the selection of planes and contours and their non-naturalistic recomposition.

But if the cubists had been interested in breaking up forms to reorganize compositionally in their paintings, Chagall was primarily interested in breaking up memories. Just as he reorganized various units from his recollections of Vitebsk into a non-naturalistic composite in *I and the Village*, he followed the same procedure with minor variations in his view of the Champ de Mars, *Paris Through the Window* (page 28). In the same years he also returned to what seem almost direct memories of his boyhood. In a painting such as *The Cattle Dealer* (above) we are recalled to his autobiography where he says "I have forgotten to remember you, little Uncle Neuch. With you I used to go out into the country to look for cattle. How happy I was when you consented to take me in your jolting cart!"

SIMPLICITY AND CRAFT

Chagall always manages to give the impression of keeping a child's innocence of eye. Yet if we consider *The Cattle Dealer* (above) closely we will realize that what Paul Valéry said of La Fontaine also applies here. "Carelessness here is expert; laxity, studied; ease the height of art. As for naïvete, that of course is to be dismissed. Such sustained skill and innocence, to my mind,

The Pregnant Woman. 1913. Oil, 76⅜ x 45⅞". Municipal Museum, Amsterdam. Regnault Collection.

preclude any indolence or 'simplicity.' "* For here we see a repetition, or rather a development of the cross-canvas compositional device to emphasize the plane of picture surface, which he had employed in the second *Wedding*. Here he further exaggerates the effect by omitting the wheels on the far side of the cart in order to give the vehicle as little depth as possible. Stress likewise is placed on curves and angles parallel to the plane of the picture surface. Even the profile treatment of the principal figures recalls the conventions of primitive fresco painters—notably the walking figure, with its obvious reminiscence of the figure of the Good Shepherd, and the head of

* Paul Valéry, *Variété*, Paris, N.R.F. 1924, p. 56. Quoted by Cassou, bibl. 40, pp. 68-9.

Paris through the Window. 1913. Oil, 52¼ x 54¾″. The Solomon R. Guggenheim Foundation, New York.

the beast so carefully composing and accenting the corner of the rectangle, yet carrying the observer's eye back into the picture.

Again in the *Pregnant Woman* (page 27) we have an adaptation of tradition to phantasy in its reminiscence of the *Blacherniotissa*,† the famous Byzantine Virgin with the figure of Christ, framed medalion-fashion, in her breast, from which so many well-known Russian ikons, such as the Madonnas of Igor, Kostroma, Novgorod and Kurssk, took their inspiration.

† Bazin, bibl. 91, p. 321.

APOLLINAIRE AND WALDEN

Another important figure in the Paris world in which Chagall had come to feel so much at home, was Guillaume Apollinaire. Apollinaire was the friend and spokesman of the cubists, as well as the leading poet of the younger generation. As a companion, an artist, a champion, he was liked and admired on all sides.

Chagall, because he did not adhere closely to the cubist view, felt Apollinaire could not sympathize with his work. Though he had known him for some time he was hesitant to bring him to his studio. One evening after dinner, he and Apollinaire walked back to La Ruche together. Chagall explained his views. For him impressionism, cubism, symbolism, realism, were only so much formal baggage. "Primitive art already had a technical perfection towards which the present generation is striving, now playing tricks of sleight of hand, now falling into stylization. I compare this formal baggage to the Pope of Rome sumptuously vested beside Christ naked, or to the lavishly decorated church beside prayer in the open fields."

Apollinaire listened, sat down and muttered something about "supernatural." The next day Chagall received a letter enclosing a poem dedicated to him.

Another evening Chagall was with a group at Apollinaire's. The poet turned to a little man in the corner. "Do you know what you must do, Mr. Walden? You must put on an exhibition of the work of this young man. Don't you know him? Chagall . . ."

In June of that year, 1914, Chagall was in Berlin for the opening of the exhibition arranged by Herwarth Walden, editor of *Der Sturm*, in the two little rooms in the Potsdammerstrasse where he edited the review. This was Chagall's first one-man exhibition. And the introduction to the catalog was the poem by Apollinaire:

ROTSOGE

Au peintre Chagall

Ton visage écarlarte ton biplan transformable en hydroplan
Ta maison ronde où il nage un hareng saur
Il me faut la clef des paupières
Heureusement que nous avons vu M. Panado
Et nous sommes tranquilles de ce côté-la
Qu'est-ce que tu veux mon vieux M. D.
90 ou 324 un homme en l'air un veau qui regarde à travers le
ventre de sa mère
J'ai cherché longtemps sur les routes
Tant d'yeux sont clos au bord des routes
Le vent fait pleurer les saussaies
Ouvre ouvre ouvre ouvre ouvre
Regarde mais regarde donc
Le vieux se lave les pieds dans la cuvette
Una volta to inteso dire Ach du lieber Gott
Et je me pris à pleurer en me souvenant de nos enfances
Et toi tu me montres un violet épouvantable

Ce petit tableau où il y a une voiture m'a rappelé le jour
Un jour fait de morceaux mauves jaunes bleus verts et rouges
Ou je m'en allais à la campagne avec une charmante cheminée tenant sa chienne en laisse
J'avais un mirliton que je n'aurais pas échangé contre un bâton de maréchal de France
Il n'y en a plus je n'ai plus mon petit mirliton
La cheminée fume loin de moi des cigarettes russes
Sa chienne aboie contre les lilas
Et la veilleuse consumée
Sur la robe ont chu des pétales
Deux anneaux d'or près des sandales
Au soleil se sont allumés
Tandis que tes cheveux sont comme le trolley
A travers l'Europe vêtue de petits feux multicolores.

Translation on page 102.

Burning House. 1913. Oil, 42 x 47¼". Collection Frau Nell Urech-Walden, Schinznach-Bad, Switzerland.

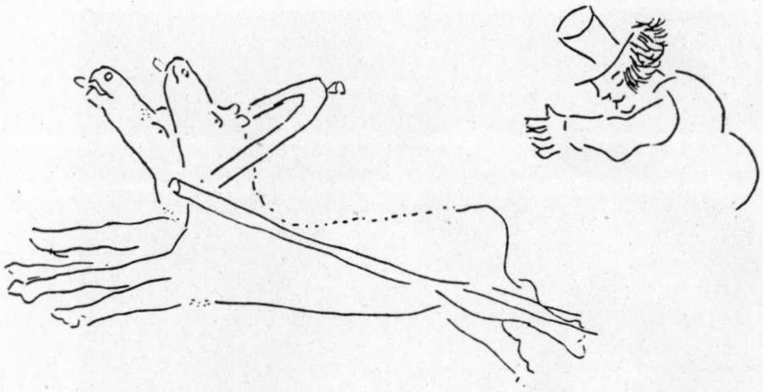

RETURN TO RUSSIA 1914

From Berlin to Vitebsk was only a step. Chagall had no notion of the impending disaster. But he had scarcely arrived in his native town when the border was closed. It was eight years and more before he saw Paris again.

If the exposure to cubism had effected both a formal liberation in his work and a distinctly personal approach to his subject matter, it had also afforded a discipline. The result is clear from a comparison of his 1914 *Self-Portrait* (page 32), painted shortly after his return, with his earlier *Portrait of My Fiancée in Black Gloves* (page 10). The soft contour lines of the earlier painting have now given way to an austere outline. The rectangle of the picture space is now tightly organized—the suggestion of atmospheric space round the figure in the earlier pictures having been replaced by color planes functioning almost as forms in the total composition. *Self-Portrait* may appear superficially much further from the cubist outlook than such a painting as *Homage to Apollinaire, Cendrars, Canudo and Walden*, 1911-12 (page 23). But the increased compositional confidence and economy of form are clearly the result of his total Paris practice.

During his first months in Vitebsk a new factualism and reserve began to appear in his work. In Paris, from the days of his arrival there, he had dreamed of Russia. Throughout those years he had been able to visualize the little world of his youth only from steadily paling memories. Now that he was back in the midst of it, he seemed to feel an impelling need to record it at once, directly, almost literally, in order to be able to keep it with him afterwards, fixed on canvas. There is, for example, the portrait of his sister, *Lisa with a Mandolin* (page 33), several homely domestic studies such as the brooding hen in a box on the floor, or a family group around a table. He found a beggar and paid him a few kopecks to pose in the phylacteries and thalis of the *Praying Jew* (page 35), and on another occasion an itinerant preacher—"the preacher of Slouzsk"—served as model for the *Old Man in Green*. In this phase of his work his interest in illogical associations of detail and ambiguities of scale seems to have temporarily disappeared. And when both reappear shortly afterwards, with the tiny figure on the head of the man wearing the prayer shawl in *Feast Day* (page 34), and in the beggar, with bag and sticks, floating through the sky in *Suburbs*

Self-Portrait. 1914. Oil. Collection Charles Im Obersteg, Basel, Switzerland.

of Vitebsk, they are reinforced by a more pervasive realism than is found in any of his Paris paintings.

In 1915 Chagall married Bella, the "fiancée in black gloves" of his early Vitebsk days. Marriage; a few days in the country; then his class was called up for military duty. He was entrained for Petrograd but there he was fortunate enough to find a desk job in a government office under his brother-in-law.

Thanks to this chance, painting was not impossible though the opportunities were limited. In the 1915 Moscow Art Salon he exhibited twenty-four paintings; and the following year in the exhibition of the Jack of Diamonds group, with such painters as Altman, Kliun, Popova, Puni, Malevich, Rozanova and Udaltzova, he was represented by fifty pictures painted in Russia since his return from Paris. In Petrograd he was also fortunate in finding companions who would talk painting with him, notably the physician-author Baal-Machschowess-Eljacheff, whom he met at the home of the collector Kagan-Chabchaj. This circle was passionately interested in the new developments in art that were taking place on all sides in spite of the war. And Kagan-Chabchaj, who was one of the first amateurs of Chagall's paintings, had even begun building up a collection of them as a nucleus for a national museum.

In February 1917 came the revolution. First the provisional government; then Kerensky; then Korniloff; finally Lenin. Shortly after the October Revolution, at a meeting of actors and painters there was talk of establishing a Ministry of the Arts. Chagall's name was proposed for the post. But he decided that if he were to be a minister it would be better to be one in his native town. He left Petrograd at once for Vitebsk. He was appointed. And the ministry was to be a stormy and ungrateful one for him.

MINISTER OF ART, VITEBSK 1917

One good feature of the appointment however was the fact that it allowed him to return to his native town. But instead of going back to his easel he set about founding a school of fine arts. He had known Lunatcharsky, the new People's Commissar for Public Instruction, as a newspaper man in Paris. And what money he now got for the support of his school was through Lunatcharsky's assistance. But times were very hard. It was difficult for the commissars to whom he had to appeal for supplies to see any urgency in his requests when the whole country required aid. Furthermore, Chagall was probably less an administrator than a painter. One day when he was out of town endeavoring to raise funds, a revolt, led by the painter Malevich, broke out among the professors, and Chagall was free of his official duties to return once again to his own work.

In 1915 he had painted the first of what was to become a long series of paintings of lovers,

Lisa with a Mandolin. 1914. Oil, 15 x 19¾". Owned by the artist.

Feast Day. 1914. Oil. Collection Charles Im Obersteg, Basel, Switzerland.

Opposite: The Praying Jew (The Rabbi of Vitebsk). 1914. Oil, 46 x 35″. The Art Institute of Chicago, The Joseph Winterbotham Collection.

The Birthday. 1915-23. Oil, 31⅞ x 39⅜″. The Solomon R. Guggenheim Foundation, New York.

each celebrating an anniversary of his marriage with Bella, her birthday, or his or their daughter, Ida's. And from then on throughout his work this theme of marital affection and comradeship was to share his sentimental attention with the recollections of his birthplace. Even in *The Mirror* (page 38) painted in Petrograd, with the small lonely figure of Bella burying her face on the table, he seems to recall the "large mirror, hanging free, alone and cold, glittering bizarrely" in the large dark drawing-room of his house in Vitebsk. In the 1917 *Promenade* (page 39) the blithely floating figure of Bella expresses their happiness. At the same time, from a strictly pictorial point of view, it serves to fill the empty space in the upper right-hand corner of the canvas and balance compositionally the picnic spread on the ground.

In 1917 and 1918 he also returned to studies of his native city (page 40) and painted some of his strongest and most dramatic landscapes. In *Gate to the Cemetery* there are still survivals of

The Mirror. 1916. Oil. Russian state collection.

cubist interests. But now the geometrical emphases are used to suggest a dramatic overtone, rather than to stress the plane of the picture's surface. A hardness and coldness are the dominant notes. The crisp contour lines are matched by a precision of brushwork. There is none of the apparent impetuosity and swinging rhythms of that earlier emotional work, *Dedicated to My Fiancée;* likewise the sultry colors of that painting have now given way to deep mineral blues and greens. In *Cemetery* (page 42) of the same year an emotional evocation is also clearly the artist's aim. But here his colors are muted. It is as if he felt that a staccato interplay of lines and broken forms and the associations of his subject were sufficient and that subdued grays and pale earth reds were the complexion of his mood. And in these two canvases Chagall may be said to have attained the maturity of his dramatic expressionism with a control and restraint which he did not command at the time of his Parisian work in this vein.

And in 1917, the same year as these landscapes, we see what may be evidence of a return to

Promenade. 1917. Oil. The State Russian Museum, Leningrad.

The Market Place. c. 1917. Oil, 26 x 38¼″. On anonymous loan to the Worcester Museum.

The Man with a Load of Mischief. 18th century English inn sign attributed to Hogarth.

Self-Portrait with Wineglass (Double Portrait). 1917. Oil, 92½ x 54″.
Pierre Matisse Gallery, New York.

Cemetery. 1917. Oil, 27¼ x 39½″. Owned by the artist.

a still earlier interest—the interest in shop signs which had led him to apprentice himself to a sign painter in his early days in St. Petersburg. For in *Self-Portrait with Wineglass* (page 41) there appears a possible iconographic relationship to the famous English inn sign *The Man with a Load of Mischief* (page 40), rather questionably attributed to Hogarth. The derivation may have been indirect, or from a common ancestor, and very likely unconscious. But the similarities of composition, theme and details are striking.

Fritz Endell in a chapter on artists as sign painters in his book, *Old Tavern Signs*, writes: "Among English artists . . . Hogarth deserves first place. He is supposed to be the author of a sign, not very gallant to the fair sex, called *A Man Loaded with Mischief* . . . I doubt if Hogarth engraved this plate himself; it is signed 'Sorrow' as the engraver and 'Experience' as the designer."

And just as Hogarth's keen observation of street signs is clear from his frequent use of them in his London engravings Chagall's interest in them is evidenced in another 1917 painting *The Market Place* (page 40) by the prominence he gives the large mineral water signboard in the picture's foreground.

The Green Violinist. 1918. Oil, 77 x 42½″. The Solomon R. Guggenheim Foundation, New York.

Study for *Introduction to the New Theatre,* principal mural in the State Jewish Theatre, Moscow. In the disk at the left appears Chagall, carried by the critic Efross and preceded by Granovsky.

MOSCOW STATE JEWISH THEATRE 1919

But the art which had made the greatest progress in Russia since the revolution was the theatre. It had always attracted Chagall. In 1911 the critic, Tugendhold, had pointed out in a review that Chagall had put such vitality into his paintings that he should be able to produce striking psychological sets. He had even suggested to Tairov that Chagall design sets for a production of *The Merry Wives of Windsor,* though nothing came of it. In 1917 Chagall had made several curtain designs and a stage set for a Gogol festival at the experimental Hermitage Theatre in Petrograd. And once he was officially released from his directorship of the academy in Vitebsk he turned to the stage and to Moscow.

At the time Granovsky was planning a new Jewish Theatre and remodeling a small hall to house it. This had originally been the drawing-room of an apartment. From it came the name State Jewish Kamerny, or Chamber, Theatre. Funds were very scarce; but Granovsky was more interested in building a company than in a pretentious installation.

Granovsky put the Jew on the stage with all his racial color and idiosyncrasies emphasized even to the point of grotesqueness. His aim was to transmute the traits of ordinary life into dramatic form by an exaggeration and stylization of gesture rhythms, speech rhythms and color, much as Synge and Lady Gregory had done a few years earlier with the colloquial idiom of the West of Ireland peasantry. And the new theatre, in contrast to the naturalist and realist theatre of Stanislavsky, was to emphasize the illogical and fantastic. The critic Efross suggested Chagall as the artist most suited to decorate the small hall in this spirit and to design the sets for the inaugural program. Granovsky commissioned Chagall to do the work, and the hall eventually became known as the "Shagalovsky Sal," the Chagall Room, or sometimes, on account of its small size, the "Chagall Box."

Detail of mural in the State Jewish Theatre. 1920. The standing figure represents the actor, Michoels, dressed as Hamlet.

As decorations for the drawing-room-auditorium Chagall painted four panels, a long mural and a frieze. The mural ran the length of the room from the entrance doors at one end to the stage at the other and was an allegory of the *Introduction to the New Theatre* (page 44). It depicted Efross carrying Chagall at once from Vitebsk to Moscow and more immediately from the entrance doors toward the stage. Further along were represented Granovsky and his leading actor, Michoels, and with them musicians, dancers, clowns and acrobats—reminders of the playful character of the new theatre in contrast to the moralizing naturalist style, a spirit closer to the *Commedia dell' Arte* than to the conventional productions of Chekhov or Gorki.

The opposite wall was broken by three windows. Between the windows were four single figure panels. These represented the folk ancestors of the four arts synthesized in the new Jewish theatre: poetry by a copyist of the Thora; acting by a Jewish wedding entertainer, the descendant of the royal entertainer of the past (page 47); music by a street violinist; and dance by a buxom girl,

Detail of mural in the State Jewish Theatre. 1920.

who, with an echo of Chagall's Chasidic upbringing, dances out of pure love and joy (page 47). Above the windows ran a long narrow frieze representing a banquet table laid for a wedding feast (page 47).

Facing the stage between the two entrance doors Chagall depicted the modern couple who dance on the stage with abandon—a relatively geometrical design in blue, gray and black to contrast with the color and activity of the side panels. The loosely hung curtain was black. And the ceiling was conceived as a sort of mirror in an interwoven pattern of grays, blacks and whites, suggesting a reflection of the colors and forms on all sides and beneath it.

Chagall's designs for Granovsky's first production—dramatizations of three stories by the Yiddish humorist, Sholom Aleichem—were his first executed theatre work. The stage sets for the three plays were, in comparison with the murals, relatively simple, although each was marked by the stylistic idiosyncrasies familiar in his paintings, particularly *Congratulations* (page 48). The results of his work had a wide repercussion in the Soviet theatre world of the day and maintained

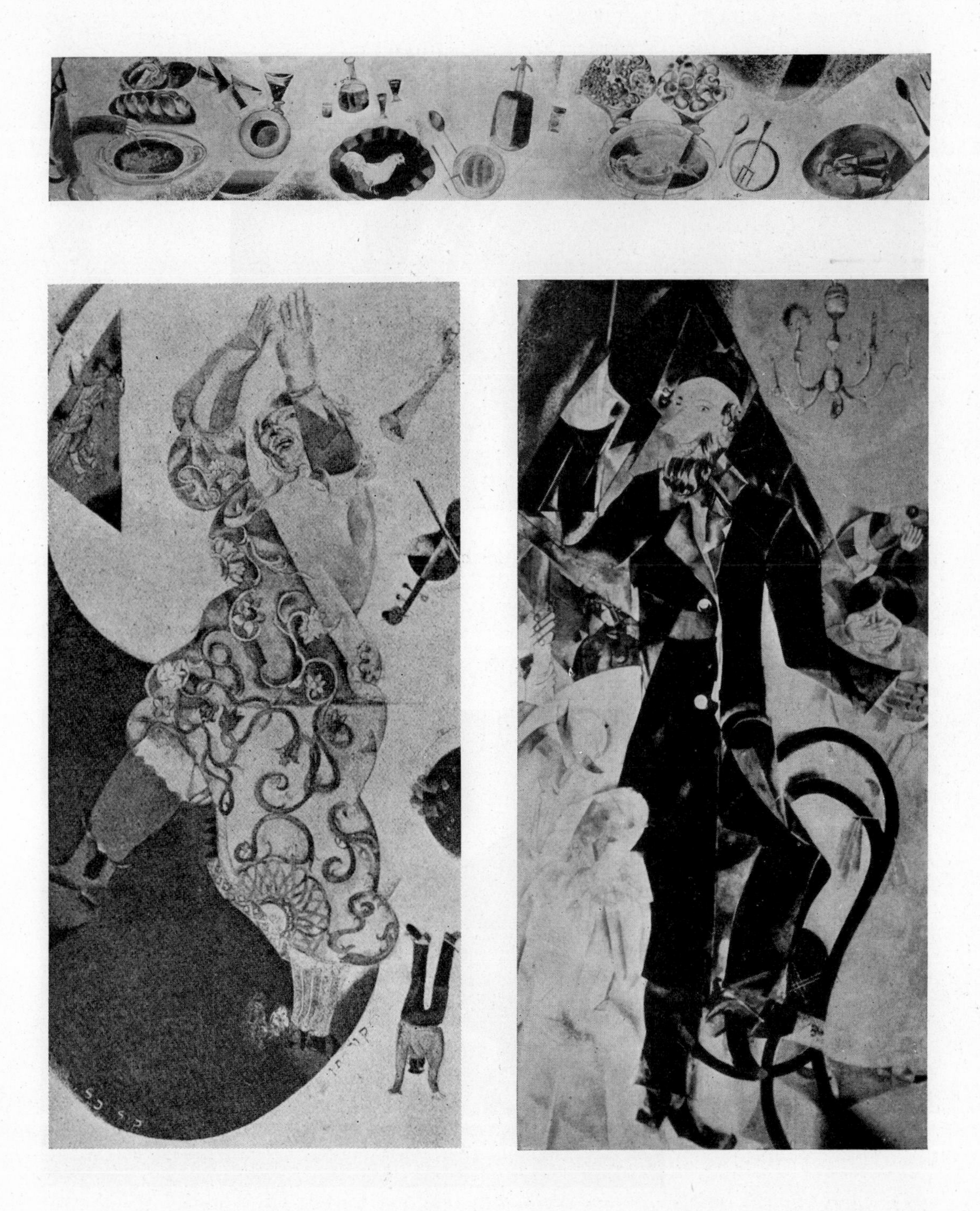

Above: The Wedding Feast. 1920. Mural frieze in the State Jewish Theatre. *Left:* The Dancing Girl. 1920. Mural panel. *Right:* The Wedding Entertainer. 1920. Mural panel.

Michoels in the rôle of Reb Alter in Sholom Aleichem's *Congratulations*, produced at the State Jewish Theatre, 1921.

Stage set design for *Congratulations*. 1919. Mixed medium, 18¾ x 24¾″. Owned by the artist.

an indirect influence there for many years. It is evident even in the constructivist settings for the *Voyage of Benjamin III*, and *200,000*, produced by Granovsky in 1923. While still associated with the State Jewish Theatre, he was approached by Vachtangov, Granovsky's rival, to design sets for a production of *The Dybbuk* at the Habima Theatre. But at the time Chagall's humor was still too unconventional for Vachtangov. And a year later, for the Second Moscow Art Theatre, Chagall designed a set for Synge's *Playboy of the Western World* which was rejected because of its fantasy, so out of keeping with the realist style which dominated that theatre.

Two years after completing his work for the State Jewish Theatre Chagall was still unpaid. During that period he had written his autobiography which appeared eleven years later in Paris as *Ma Vie*. But he had grown restive in Moscow. His friend the poet Rubiner, had written him from Germany, "Are you alive? The story goes that you were killed in the war. Do you know you are famous here? Your pictures have created expressionism. They sell very high."

Finally, with the assistance of the poet, Demian Bedny, and Lunatcharsky he succeeded in obtaining a permit to leave the Soviet Union for Paris.

RETURN TO BERLIN, 1922. "MEIN LEBEN"

Berlin was the first stop. When he left there for Vitebsk in 1914 his most important paintings were on exhibition in the offices of *Der Sturm*. On his return he found practically all had been sold and the money owed him amounted to almost nothing at the current value of the mark.

During the nine months he remained in the German capital he painted no pictures. He did, however, produce a series of engravings for an edition of his autobiography, *Mein Leben*, which Paul Cassirer was to publish. In the end the publication of the text was abandoned in favor of a portfolio of dry points under the same title (page 77). Cassirer issued it, as well as several other plates of similar character independent of the portfolio.

But Chagall's Berlin sojourn was not, however, to be all disappointments for him. As his friend Rubiner had pointed out, Chagall's reputation had grown remarkably in Western Europe during his eight years in Russia. Although he had gained nothing financially from all the paintings he had left behind him in Berlin, he had gained much in the way of recognition. Already in 1914 he had warm admirers in Germany among the younger men. Heinrich Campendonck, one of those associated with the Blue Rider group, had been notably influenced. A still younger man, Max Ernst, recalls having been so struck by a reproduction of *To Russia, Asses and Others* that when he got to Berlin in 1916 he went directly to the gallery of *Der Sturm* to see what remained of the Chagall exhibition. And the influence of Chagall is readily recognizable in certain Ernsts as late as 1919. Again, in Belgium he was highly regarded by the second generation of the Laetham-Saint-Martin group—Servaes, Permeke, Gustave de Smet, and by Edgard Tytgat, who four years later, when the group gave a party on the river Lys in Chagall's honor, was to celebrate the event in his painting *Remembrance of a Sunday*.*

* Reproduced in Jean Milo, *Edgard Tytgat*, Paris, 1930, pl. 12.

Two months before leaving Paris for Berlin in 1914 Charles Malpel, an attorney who also dealt privately in paintings, had arranged a contract with Chagall through Cendrars paying him 250 francs monthly for seven small pictures. Only two months of this contract had elapsed before his departure. But after Chagall had been cut off in Russia by the outbreak of the war Malpel continued to draw on the stock of paintings left behind by Chagall in La Ruche with the intention of paying Chagall the accumulated monthly amounts on his return. At this same time, several of Chagall's neighbors made free with the paintings left in the studio and the critic, Gustave Coquiot, unaware of the manner in which they had been acquired, purchased several of the canvases. Ambroise Vollard had seen some of these paintings at Coquiot's and had immediately requested his address.

Chagall lost no time in leaving for Paris. And shortly afterwards it was agreed that he should prepare a series of etchings to illustrate a Vollard edition of Gogol's *Dead Souls*.

Blue House. 1920. Oil, 26⅛ x 38¼". The Museum of Fine Arts, Liège, Belgium.

PARIS AND GOGOL'S "DEAD SOULS"

Chagall was the perfect choice as illustrator of Gogol's novel. He was familiar with a provincial corner of Russia very similar to the setting which Gogol had given Chitchikov's rascalities; he had also a sentimental attachment to it, and a sense of humor. As a result, though he was keenly aware of the foibles of the provincial life which he had to depict, he would neither treat it with too sharp a satire, nor fail to bring out its faults. This is what we find in the hundred odd plates, tail pieces and ornamental initials that would have made a masterpiece of illustration had the book not remained unpublished like so many other Vollard projects. In the three years he worked at it, Chagall had gradually won a new fluidity of line and a sensibility to tonal contrasts that were shortly to influence his oils by softening the severity of line and the bold, often strident, colors which had characterized his later Russian period.

During these three years Chagall had also gradually found his way back into Parisian life. In 1924 the Galerie Barbazanges-Hodebert held an exhibition of his work from the years 1908 to 1921. French taste, however, in its rationality and decorum still found Chagall's illogicalities of representation difficult to accept. And in spite of the recognition of Rouault and the growing acknowledgment of Soutine, dramatic and sentimental emphases so popular in expressionistic centers found little favor. It is true that several younger admirers of Giorgio de Chirico were beginning to make themselves heard. But even these future surrealists did not, as Breton confesses, become aware of the kinship between many facets of Chagall's work and their own aims until much later.

In spite of this lack of recognition from the French, however, Paris still remained for Chagall "his second birthplace." And little by little the atmospheric mildness of the Ile de France and the Riviera began to modify his earlier asperity. Now instead of those constant nostalgic dreams of his first visit we find him more often applying his technique of mellowed tonalities to the French countryside as in *Landscape* (page 54). Even in paintings whose subjects may still draw their inspiration from boyhood recollection, such as *The Trough* (page 55), there is a softening of forms, a melting of contour lines in the general atmosphere of the canvas and an interest in subtleties of texture which did not exist in his paintings of five years earlier.

Double Portrait. 1924. Oil, 51¼ x 37⅜″. Collection Philippe Dotremont, Uccle-Brussels, Belgium.

Marc Chagall with his wife and daughter in his Paris studio, 1924. Photograph Thérèse Bonney.

THE FABLES OF LA FONTAINE

And if Vollard was intuitive in his first assignment to Chagall, he was bold as well as right in his second. For in 1926, even before the plates for *Dead Souls* were finished, he asked him to illustrate another work, *The Fables of La Fontaine.*

Perhaps the idea was suggested to him by one of the Gogol plates, *The Barn Yard* (page 78). At any rate this subject matter was just as congenial to Chagall as the provincial Russian setting of the former book. Animals had figured persistently in his painting since his early years. And his depictions of them always had a homely, sympathetic character.

Yet when Vollard held an exhibition of the preliminary gouache illustrations, at the Galerie Bernheim-jeune in February 1930, there was a violent critical outburst. It was claimed that Vollard had shown not only very poor judgment but also poor taste in commissioning Chagall, a romantic and an oriental, to illustrate these classical 17th century French masterpieces. The protest had undoubtedly xenophobic and possibly anti-Semitic inspirations. Aside from Chagall's

Landscape. Ile Adam, 1925. Collection Mme Fontaine, Paris.

proven talents as an illustrator and his sympathetic vision of the animal world, which alone would recommend him for the choice, there was a very live fabulist tradition in Russia in Chagall's boyhood. For Krylov, one of the most popular Russian classic authors during the 19th century, owed his reputation as the first Russian poet of national importance to his fables. The earliest fables of Krylov are translations of La Fontaine's, or at least recreations of them.

Vollard's first plan was to have Chagall make color engravings in the 18th century manner. Chagall set to work on a hundred gouaches for this purpose. Vollard had a special studio built for the work, to be directed by the artisan-engraver Maurice Potin, who had several Prix de Rome winners among his workmen. Many color experiments were made. But in the end the results were unsatisfactory. There were too many gradations of tone in the gouaches. The work of reproducing them suitably would be endless. Vollard decided to abandon the project—but not the illustration of *The Fables*. He commissioned Chagall to do the same number of plates in

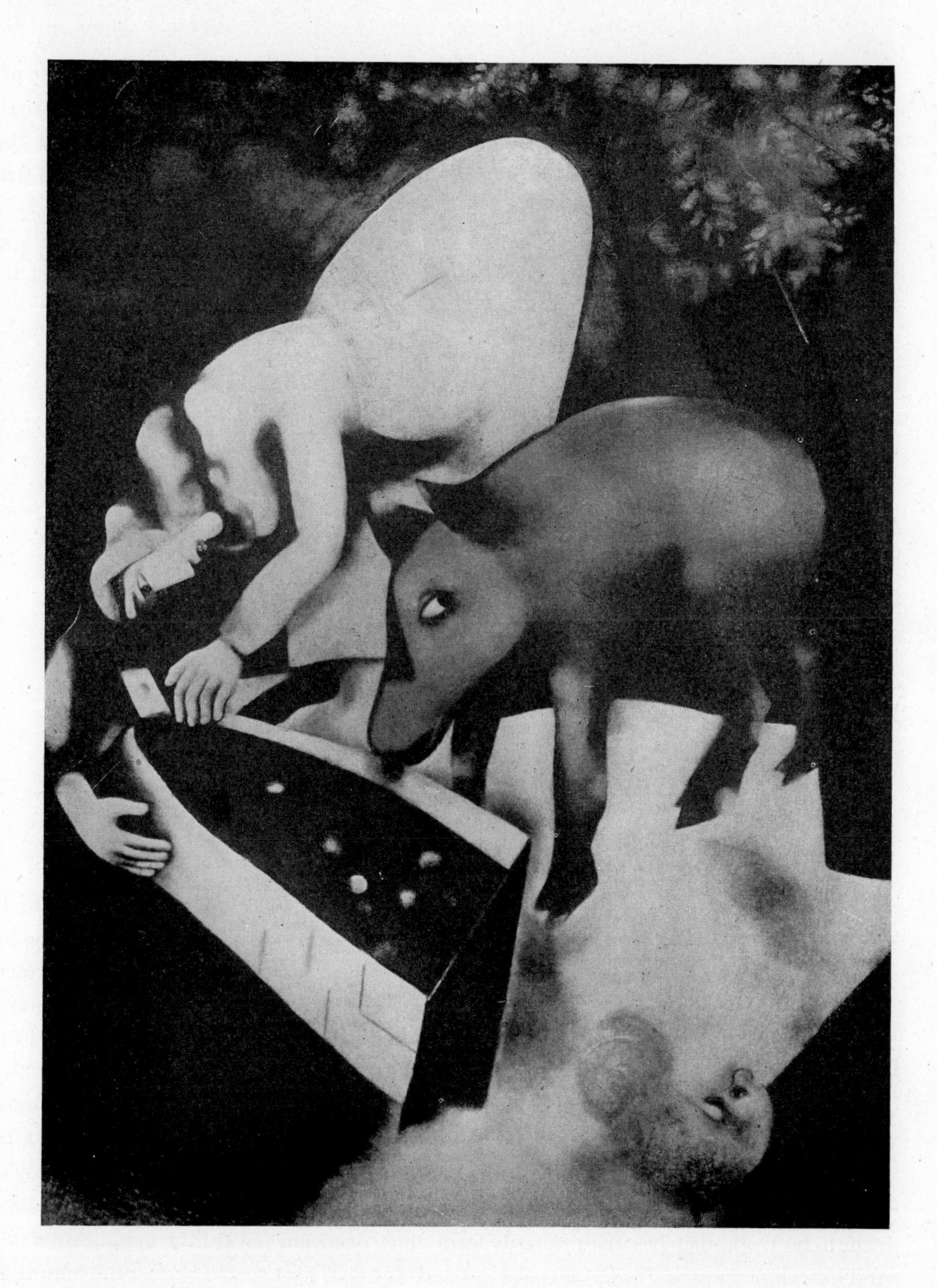

The Trough. 1925. Oil, 57⅝ x 45⅛″. Collection the Vicomte de Noailles, Paris.

black and white. Finally, after three changes of engraver, the destruction of one complete printing and a remaking of all the plates, the work, which was begun in 1927, was completed in 1931.

The final result even surpassed *Dead Souls* in quality. It has been said of Chagall "he likes color, but prefers light." In these prints there is a notable increase in luminosity and delicacy. Both are peculiarly suited to the subject matter. The sharp line of his earlier work was appropriate to Gogol's satire; but the sentiment and sympathy of La Fontaine demanded a subtler touch. And the general atmospheric enrichment and deeper interest in subtleties of texture, recognizable in his oils of the same period, provided it.

FLOWERS

A new note now began to assert itself in the subject matter of his pictures. It was in Toulon in 1924, Chagall recalls, that the charm of French flowers first struck him. He claims he had not known bouquets of flowers in Russia—or at least they were not so common as in France. The event undoubtedly had its important associations in his world of sentiment. He has said that when he painted a bouquet it was as if he were painting a landscape. It represented France to him. But the discovery was also a logical one in the light of the change taking place in his vision and pictorial interests. Flowers, especially mixed bouquets of tiny blossoms, offer a variety of delicate color combinations and a fund of texture contrasts which were beginning to hold Chagall's attention more and more. To him they may have had a sentimental origin, as the lovers in his "anniversary" pictures undoubtedly had. But very soon, like every other representational element in his work, they became primarily form units, or means toward the organization of forms. And in such pictures as *The Circus* (page 57) and *The Bride with the Double Face* the minute texture details soon became fused into a compositional unity by the soft luminous atmosphere in which he wraps them.

On his return to France Chagall lived with his wife and daughter in a studio at 36, Avenue

The Circus. 1926. Oil, 46 x 35″. Collection Dr. Potvin, Brussels.

In the Mountain. 1930. Oil, 28 x 23″. Collection Mr. and Mrs. Joseph Bissett, New York.

d'Orléans, on the same court in which Lenin had hidden on his way to Russia. Two years later the family moved to Boulogne-sur-Seine. And from then on each vacation found them in a different part of France—Savoie, Auvergne, the Pyrenees, the Riviera. Through all this period one feels a happiness, a joy of living in his work. Animals, lovers, flowers; his series of circus gouaches; or vacation landscapes at Peira Cava near Nice (above). Now, there was none of that longing of his first Paris years for something beyond reach, or that melancholy and inquietude of his Russian paintings. Instead each new picture seemed to exude a warmer sentimental glow, as much a product of the technique of which he was gaining constantly a fuller mastery as of his subject matter.

In 1931 the autobiography which he had written during his last two years in Russia was published in Paris as *Ma Vie*. It was illustrated by early drawings instead of the engravings which he had originally made for the text. But shortly afterwards he had another call from Vollard for illustrations—fitted to his tastes and talents—a Vollard edition of the Bible.

The Lovers in the Flowers (Lilacs). 1931. Oil, 51 x 35″. Collection Josef von Sternberg, Hollywood.

Solitude. 1933. Oil, 43⅝ x 66″. Owned by the artist.

PRESENTIMENTS

As a preparation for this work he decided in 1931 to make a trip to the Near East, Egypt, Syria, Palestine. In the course of his journey he painted a series of landscapes notable for a meticulous documentary character, which nevertheless does not interfere with a distinctive emotional overtone. While the subject matter and technical treatment in a painting such as *The Wailing Wall* are completely different from his Vitebsk realist paintings of 1914, there is a certain kinship between these two phases of his work. Just as the playfulness of his first Paris work had been supplanted by a greater thoughtfulness on his return to his native environment, now the light-hearted sentiment of his Peira Cava landscapes and the carefree work of the twenties have given way to a melancholy expression. And freedom from anxiety is rarely to show itself during the next decade.

In fact with a painting such as *Solitude* (above) an air of spiritual foreboding begins to appear in his work, as if something within him were sensitive to developments which on all sides were preparing the way for the tragedy still six years off.

During the same years his restlessness increased. In 1932 he made a trip to Holland to study Rembrandt. In 1933 he attended the opening of his large retrospective exhibition in Basel. In

1934 he went to Spain to study El Greco; in 1935 to Poland; in 1937 to Italy and the primitives.

And in the paintings of this period we find his old themes returning. Haunted by his forebodings and in the midst of the general European discontent, he seemed to turn back for reassurance to his recollections of Vitebsk. These pictures of the middle thirties are composed much as were those of his early nostalgic phase; but he is now quite far from the cubist insistence on the composition of the picture plane. This is replaced by the new atmospheric and textural interests of his recent landscape studies.

In *Nude over Vitebsk* we have the square and the great white church of St. Elias. The nude, used "to fill the empty space" of the sky, is possibly a recollection of his fiancée posing for him, which he describes in his memoirs. In another canvas we have a view of his home and "the stoop-shouldered beggar with his sack on his back and his stick in hand" composed with two vases of flowers out of the twenties. In *Time is a River Without Banks* (page 65) appear the huge clock, which recurs so insistently in early drawings and paintings, the inevitable lovers and a herring which his father's work would never permit him to forget. And in *The Bride and Groom of the Eiffel Tower* (page 68) he brings a whole sequence of events into one composition in the primitive convention.

The other aspect of his work in these years is nourished by his steadily increasing "presentiments." From *Solitude* these forebodings of evil or warnings of impending disaster take a more dramatic turn in *Crucifixion* of 1938 (page 62); and become colored by social alarms in *Revolution* of two years later.

WORK ON THE BIBLE

All this time the work on the Bible illustrations had progressed. On his return from Palestine, Chagall had made about twenty sketches for the book of Genesis to feel his way compositionally. He then started at once on the definitive plates. And by the time of Vollard's death in July 1939 he had completed 105 plates of the series.

Like the preliminary gouache and oil sketches, in which he had employed the same motives

White Crucifixion. 1938. Oil, 61 x 55″. Owned by the artist.

he intended to use in his plates, these engravings were much closer in character and technique to his Palestine landscapes than anything that had gone before. The forms were more fully modeled than in his earlier work. The treatment of the plate was much less linear than even the *La Fontaine* illustrations. The interest in atmosphere and detail that had shown itself in his oils was now translated to the copper plate just as completely and effectively as the rich tonalities of his gouaches had been ten years earlier. And the drama and mystery of the representations came out more eloquently in his delicately modulated grays, blacks and whites than one could possibly imagine in a broad gamut of color. There is a dignity and mystery in his conceptions that lift them to one of the highest levels of his achievement to date.

In 1939 Chagall and his wife moved to Gordes, above Marseille. In September war was declared. But work with Chagall at Gordes went on practically as usual. And in February 1940 he held a large exhibition at the Galerie Mai in Paris. Four months later the Germans entered the capital. But a long year was to elapse before he finally reached New York on June 21, 1941.

NEW YORK

In spite of the trying experiences he had been through it seemed no time until Chagall found his feet. Still, for all his apparent resilience and energy, his work betrayed a definite disturbance and fatigue. Little that was fresh appeared in his painting for some time. Forms did not have the gaiety and assurance which had come to be regarded as characteristic of Chagall. His colors were not clear. There was a repetition of old conceptions, a lack of conviction.

Fortunately, in the early part of 1942, Leonide Massine invited him to design the costumes and sets for a new ballet, *Aleko*, and to supervise its production in Mexico City. An environment with fewer reminders of events in Europe and a definite job to be done were both beneficial.

On Chagall's return there was a notable clarification of his palette. The Mexican scene had added new colors and new themes to his repertory. These changes appeared first in a group of gouaches exhibited shortly after his return. But soon, in a less obvious way, they became recognizable also in the revitalized tone of more ambitious work, such as *Juggler* of 1943. Here, although Chagall returned to a combination of his Vitebsk and circus memories, the gloomy and uncertain character of his oils of the past few years was replaced by a gayer tone implicit in his bright, contrasting blues, reds and greens as well as in his subject. Once again the picture is simply an organization of recollected forms employed, as he had employed them thirty years earlier, primarily as pictorial elements to "fill empty spaces as the composition requires and according to his humor." If there is any symbolism in them, it is not intentional. Nevertheless it achieves once again that metaphorical character in its association of disparate images which, in a more direct technique, had marked his early Paris work and which Cendrars and Apollinaire found so congenial to their approach in poetry.

Another canvas of a few months later, *Listening to the Cock*, making use of a device of trans-

The Red Cock. 1940. Oil, 29 x 36″. Collection Miss Mary E. Johnston, Glendale, Ohio.

parency reminiscent of the earlier *Cattle Dealer*, is still more clearly indebted to his Mexican sojourn for its color (page 69). And recollections of the visit continue to appear in his paintings for the next year and more.

After its presentation in Mexico City the ballet *Aleko* was brought to New York. What Efross said of Chagall's work for Granovsky in Moscow was still in great part true. "He made drawings and paintings but not at all sketches for scenery or costumes. On the contrary, he transformed the performers and the spectacle into a category of pictorial art. He did not make sets, but rather panel paintings." * The backdrop seemed more like a vast painting by Chagall in front of which the performers moved than an integral part of the production and even dwarfed the dancers by its visual force. Nevertheless there was a spirit of holiday and magic in it and an exuberance of color that was Chagall at his purest.

* Bibl. 116, p. 44.

Time is a River without Banks. 1930-39. Oil on canvas, 39⅜ x 32″. The Museum of Modern Art.

The Bride and Groom of the Eiffel Tower. 1938-39. Oil, 58¾ x 54⅛″. Pierre Matisse Gallery, New York.

Listening to the Cock. 1944. Oil, 38½ x 28″. Collection Adolphe A. Juviler, New York.

Spirit of the Town. 1945. Oil, 42 x 32″. Pierre Matisse Gallery, New York.

In September, 1944, Madame Chagall died. The loss was a staggering one to Chagall. His thoughts and work for months seemed fixed irremediably on the past. Then fortunately the ballet once again was able to render a service of distraction.

The Ballet Theater was planning a revised production of Stravinsky's *Fire Bird.* On very short notice they called on Chagall for aid. A few months' intensive work and the result in the way of visual spectacle was even more impressive than *Aleko*—compositions in Chagall's most characteristic manner, with all stops out, expanded to the size of the New York Metropolitan Opera House stage. They were more like huge murals than stage sets—murals that had grown out of that panel in Granovsky's little theatre in Moscow, and, at a further remove, out of the pride with which he recalled in his autobiography his grandfather painting on the walls of the synagogue of Mohilev. More opulent than *Aleko's*, his *Fire Bird* curtains seemed a release of all those pent-up emotions and memories that had been haunting and saddening his work during the preceding months. And in the paintings that immediately followed he is once again the poet of his young days, but with a maturity of technique and a warmth and control of color he had never previously achieved.

Chagall is a conscious artist. While the selection and combination of his images may appear illogical from a representational viewpoint, they are carefully and rationally chosen elements for the pictorial structure he seeks to build. There is nothing automatic in his work. In fact his much talked of illogicality appears only when his paintings are read detail by detail; taken in the composite they have the same pictorial integrity as the most naturalistic painting, or the most architectural cubist work of the same level of quality. He is an artist with a full color sense. He has a deep regard for technique. He is a subtle craftsman who, rather than dull his hand in virtuosity, affects clumsiness. He is an artist who has been content with a limited repertory of representational forms. But his work of nearly forty years shows a persistent effort to bring out new and richer effects from his consciously limited thematic material by unaccustomed arrangements and by a steady development of a more complex technique. In an age that has fled from sentiment he has drawn constantly on it for his stimulation. And our debt to Chagall is to an artist who has brought poetry back into painting through subject matter, without any sacrifice of his painter's interest in the picture for itself, and entirely aside from any communication that can be put into words.

James Johnson Sweeney

THE PRINTS OF MARC CHAGALL

Famous though Marc Chagall is as an artist, it can hardly be said that his reputation was built up to any appreciable extent through his work as a printmaker. Yet Chagall has executed close to four hundred different subjects in various graphic media. Best known among them are the twenty plates of the autobiographic series which was published in 1923 by Paul Cassirer in Berlin under the title *Mein Leben.* A few odd plates closely connected with *Mein Leben* were issued separately by Cassirer about the same time. Then, here and there, we find a little etching of his in one book or another. And that is about all we know of Marc Chagall, one of the outstanding printmakers of the 20th century.

Chagall's career as a printmaker was closely linked to the French picture dealer and publisher Ambroise Vollard. It was Vollard who, having seen Chagall's early paintings, encouraged him to continue to make prints by commissioning him to illustrate a book. The plan, like everything conceived by Vollard, was an ambitious one. Chagall was to etch ninety-six illustrations for Gogol's *Dead Souls.* This was in 1923. But even before this first project was finished, the restless Vollard approached Chagall with another plan: he asked him to illustrate La Fontaine's *Fables.* There were to be one hundred plates, in full color. Chagall set to work and painted a series of one hundred gouaches. A special workshop was set up by Vollard. Here the tedious and complicated process of preparing the many color plates for each subject was to be carried out by a whole staff of engravers under the supervision of the master-printer Maurice Potin. But Chagall's rich and delicate color scale proved too much for the plan and the color plate project was abandoned. Not so the plan of creating one hundred illustrations for the *Fables.* Urged by Vollard, Chagall tackled the work himself and created one hundred etchings in black and white which belong among his best plates. This project was completed as far as Chagall's share was concerned in 1931.

Again, before the end of the second project, Vollard thought of a new book for Chagall to illustrate: the Bible. The artist, who was dissatisfied with his first trial plates for the set, decided he must study the actual landscape and people of the Holy Land in order to accomplish his aims. In 1931 he went to Egypt, Palestine and Syria. Then, back in Paris, he began this new set of plates on which he worked until Vollard's death in 1940. By that time he had finished a total of 105 plates.

Of each of the three sets of illustrations almost the entire editions were pulled, then stacked in warehouses awaiting completion of the typography, the book *per se.* But, through some odd quirk in Vollard's curious character, this important part of the work was never completed. Consequently these three hundred plates created for Vollard—almost three-quarters of Chagall's entire output of prints—have never come into circulation. Occasionally magazines have called attention

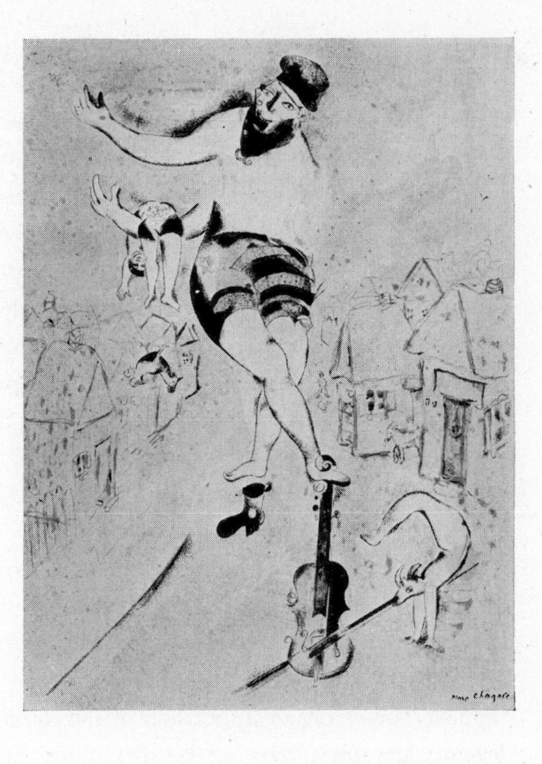

(*left*) Acrobat with Violin. 1924. Etching and drypoint, 16⅜ x 12½″. (*right*) Acrobat with Violin. 1924. Etching and drypoint with watercolor.

to Chagall's illustrations, reproducing a few, but there has never been a comprehensive exhibition of his graphic work. No public or private collection—with the exception of the artist's own—offers an opportunity to study any but the early prints of Chagall. Yet when Chagall's prints become better known he will probably prove to be one of the really great printmakers of our day.

Chagall's earliest experiments in printmaking were in woodcut and lithography. They all have a rather somber quality about them. This they never quite lose, even when brightened up with watercolor, as the artist to this day likes to do. Almost all of these early attempts remain unpublished, and there are only a few impressions of each block or stone. Neither of these media appealed to the artist, perhaps because they do not quite permit the radiance and transparency, the richness of color and tone that can be achieved on the copper plate.

Within the first year of his experiments Chagall found that etching and drypoint were his true media. In them, all that is so fantastically exuberant in his painting finds translation into terms of black and white.

His early plates, published and unpublished, some on zinc but the majority on copper, are fairly simple and direct technically. Drypoint seems to predominate, though some show etched lines to accentuate certain contours, or to bring out details. Frequently drypoint is used to work up a black surface patch and to achieve a soft contour which looks as if it had been applied with a brush. In these early prints there are few changes once the original conception has been etched or scratched into the plate. But occasionally we find later states in which radical changes in the composition have been made as in *Das Grab des Vaters* in the set of *Mein Leben*. These changes, however, are rather the exception than the rule.

The same holds true of his first set of illustrations for Vollard, Gogol's *Dead Souls*. Though quite different in composition and general approach from his earlier plates his technique has not changed greatly. We find that he uses etching more frequently; there is more pure line work. The broad brush-like contours have disappeared; broader black drypoint patches, however, occur more frequently. Nevertheless the conception appears purely graphic as color plays an insignificant part in the plate.

During this earlier period, from 1923 to 1926-27, Chagall created a small group of prints which are quite unique in their combination of etching, watercolor and drawing. He would take a few impressions of his etchings, touch them with watercolor or gouache, sometimes to such a degree that hardly anything remained of the line work. At other times he would add figures, animals, houses on an impression of the same print, completely transforming the composition, developing a story, carrying one theme into another, as in a folk-tale. They are like variations on a basic theme in which the artist gives full rein to this creative playful fantasy. Here we find the artist abandoning himself to his imagination, discarding conventions (so readily bound by a single technique) and full of whimsical ideas.

With the illustrations of La Fontaine Chagall entered into an entirely new sphere of his graphic *oeuvre*. As mentioned before, each plate was preceded by a painting in gouache. Thus these prints were conceived primarily from a painter's point of view. Black and white surfaces, reminiscent of brush strokes, dominate all line work. A broad painting-like treatment replaces the purely graphic concision and directness of much of Chagall's earlier work. A brilliance of tonality is achieved which was absent before. His technique is carried along by a burst of temperament. Where it was orthodox before—almost conventional—he now devises a system of broken surface tints (partly in aquatint), lines, scratches, dots and whatever to achieve effects similar to those in his preceding gouaches. He recreates his preliminary paintings, elaborates or simplifies them at will. But he never copies them. In his plates, however, he preserves the effect of color above all else.

The aquatint, or aquatint-like tone, is used extensively for the first time in the *Fables*. White highlights are achieved through application of stopping-out varnish with the brush. This greatly contributes to the painterly effect of these prints. In the plates themselves only minor changes seem to have been made during the etching process. Few states occur, which is not surprising since the pictorial composition had already crystallized in the preceding gouaches. When states do occur they frequently show only alterations of detail to emphasize or elaborate the story.

The Apparition of the Angel to Joshua (last state). Etching and drypoint, 11¾ x 9¼″.

Bible. 1931-39: The Apparition of the Angel to Joshua (first state). Etching and drypoint, 13⅝ x 9¾″.

In a few cases, however, the plates are first lightly etched and then undergo considerable change, not so much in the basic design as in the working out of light and shadow.

In looking over the superb set of illustrations one cannot help feeling how fortunate it was that Vollard's original plan of having color plates made after the gouaches could not be carried out. The color plates engraved by craftsmen could never have compared with Chagall's masterful re-interpretations in black and white. A certain artificiality and mechanization is inevitable in the involved color plate process. Furthermore, professional craftsmen can only copy; the artist himself recreates in translating from color to black and white.

With the illustrations for the Bible Chagall tackled his largest print enterprise. It was not only the largest in the actual number of plates but also the most elaborate and ambitious pictorially and dramatically. Again his technical approach to the problem became fundamentally different. The general tone is somber, in keeping with the emotional and dramatic content: heavy blacks and sharp contrasts of light and shadow are frequent. Many of the plates were preceded not by one but by a number of gouaches and black and white sketches. Notwithstanding these preliminary studies, almost every plate underwent a profound evolution in the course of its preparation. As many as twelve states of one plate have been found, each state showing great changes over the preceding one. At times as much as half of the composition was completely erased and reconstructed on the blank surface of the plate. Figures were added, then eliminated; an entire composition thrown into darkness where it had been light before. Throughout he made extensive use of the burnisher, polishing highlights into dark areas, evening out contrasts, adding gray tones where they had been black. Through the whole series we get the impression of a profound struggle within the artist himself, as well as a struggle with his subject and his technique. He put his entire talent as a craftsman to a final and supreme test. In none of his earlier work did he ever appear under such emotional stress and strain.

Chagall has watched the fate of his extensive, unpublished graphic work with understandable anxiety and concern. That one of the wishes closest to his heart should be the realization of his projected publications is only natural. Plans have been made to bring the three projects to the desired conclusion as soon as circumstances are more favorable.

Undaunted by these great disappointments, however, Chagall took up etching again when he came to this country. His work in Stanley William Hayter's *Studio 17* in New York has had a refreshing and vitalizing influence on his prints. He has taken up a new project: the publication of a set of subjects on the circus. It is less ambitious than the Vollard sets. Up to now twenty-five plates have been completed and Chagall plans to add others. Technically they are greatly simplified in comparison particularly with the plates for the Bible, but in them he has made some interesting experiments, particularly in the inking and printing of the plates.

Almost completely unknown to the print world, Chagall nevertheless must be regarded as one of the great etchers of our day. From the beginning he has shown a love and understanding of black and white which is unique among his contemporaries. He has never fallen into the fatal routine performance of the professional printmaker. He has always preserved the freedom of the painter and, above all else, in every one of his prints his great imagination always leads him to new and interesting results.

Carl O. Schniewind

Mein Leben. 1923: (*right*) The Grandfathers. Drypoint, 10⅞ x 8$\frac{7}{16}$″. (*below*) Pokrowa Street. Drypoint, 7$\frac{1}{16}$ x 8¼″.

Dead Souls. 1923-27: (*left*) Mme Korobotchka. Etching and drypoint, 11¾ x 8⅞″. (*below*) The Barn Yard. Etching and drypoint, 9 x 11 9/16″.

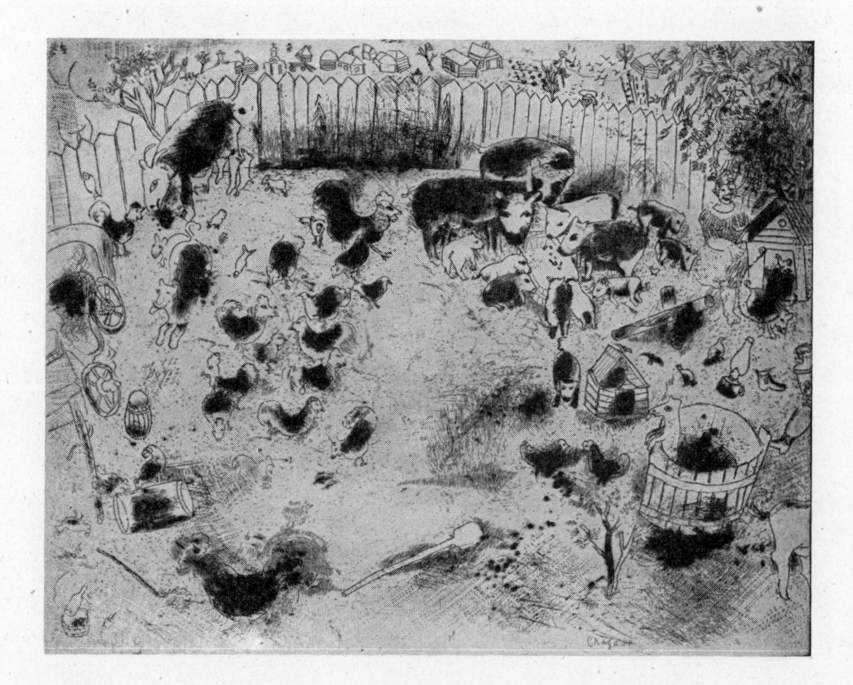

Dead Souls. 1923-27. (*left*) Chancellery. Etching and drypoint, 11 x 8¾". (*below*) Chitchikov and Sobakevitch. Etching and drypoint, 8⅜ x 10⅞".

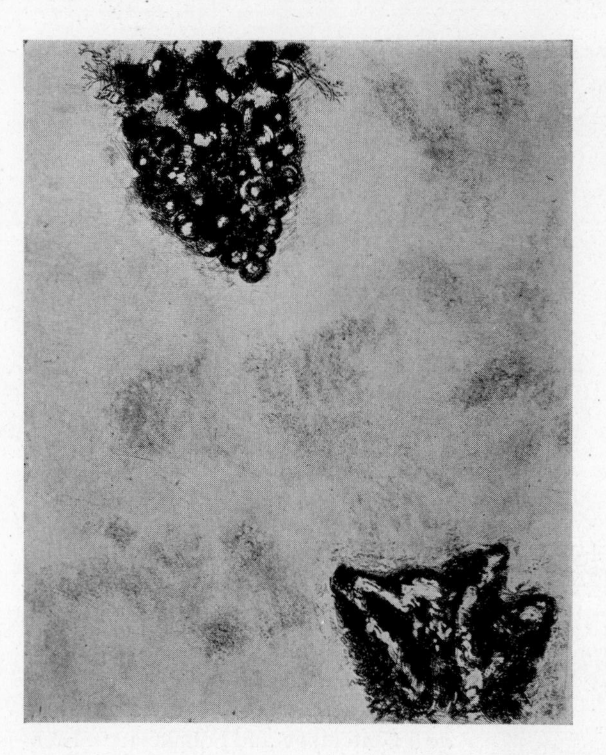

The Fables. 1927-31: The Fox and the Grapes. Etching and drypoint, 11½ x 9⁷⁄₁₆″.

The Cat Metamorphosed into a Woman. Etching and drypoint, 11⅝ x 9½″.

The Fables. 1927-31: The Two Goats. Etching and drypoint, 11⅝ x 9$\frac{5}{16}$″.

The Ass Loaded with Salt and the Ass Loaded with Sponges. Etching and drypoint, 11¾ x 9$\frac{9}{16}$″.

The Fables. 1927-31: The Lark and the Farmer. Etching and drypoint, 11⅝ x 9½″.

Bible. 1931-39: Abraham Mourns Sarah. Etching and drypoint, $11\frac{1}{2}$ x $9\frac{1}{2}$″.

Jacob's Dream. Etching and drypoint, $11\frac{5}{8}$ x $9\frac{5}{8}$″.

Bible. 1931-39: David with the Head of Goliath. Etching and drypoint, $11\frac{1}{8}$ x $9\frac{1}{2}$″.

Bible. 1931-39: Untitled (for one of the books of the Prophets). Etching and drypoint, $13\frac{5}{8}$ x $10\frac{7}{8}$″.

Bible. 1931-39: Abraham Approaching Sodom with Three Angels. Etching, 12 1/16 x 9 5/16″.

CATALOG OF THE EXHIBITION

An asterisk (*) preceding the title indicates that the work is illustrated in the text. Alternative titles are given in parenthesis; (dated) means that the date appears on the picture. In dimensions height precedes width.

Paintings

* 1 Candles in the Dark Street (La Mort). 1908 (dated). Oil on canvas, 26¾ x 34". Lent by the the artist. *Ill. p. 9.*

* 2 Portrait of My Fiancée in Black Gloves. 1909 (dated). Oil on canvas, 34¾ x 25¼". Lent by Baron Edward von der Heydt, Ascona, Switzerland. *Ill. p. 10.*

* 3 The Wedding. Paris, 1910 (dated). Oil on canvas, 39⅛ x 74¼". Lent by the artist. *Ill. p. 16.*

* 4 My Studio. Paris, 1910 (dated). Oil on canvas, 23¾ x 28¾". Lent by the artist. *Ill. p. 12.*

* 5 To Russia, Asses and Others. 1911 (dated). Oil on canvas, 61⅝ x 48⅛". Lent by the Pierre Matisse Gallery, New York. *Ill. p. 25.*

* 6 Half-Past Three (The Poet). 1911 (dated). Oil on canvas, 78 x 57". Lent by Mr. and Mrs. Walter C. Arensberg, Hollywood. *Ill. p. 17.*

* 7 I and the Village. 1911 (dated). Oil on canvas, 75⅝ x 59⅝". The Museum of Modern Art. Mrs. Simon Guggenheim Fund. *Ill. p. 19.*

8 Interior. 1911 (dated). Gouache, 7¼ x 8¼". Lent by the artist.

* 9 Dedicated to My Fiancée. 1911 (dated). Oil on canvas, 77 x 45¼". Lent by the artist. *Ill. p. 21.*

* 10 The Cattle Dealer. 1912. Oil on canvas, 38⅛ x 78⅞". Lent by Frau Nell Urech-Walden, Schinznach-Bad, Switzerland. *Ill. p. 26.*

* 11 The Soldier Drinks. 1912. Oil on canvas, 43 x 37⅛". Lent by Frau Nell Urech-Walden, Schinznach-Bad, Switzerland. *Ill. p. 22.*

* 12 The Pregnant Woman. 1913 (dated). Oil on canvas, 76⅜ x 45 ⅞". Lent by P. A. Regnault, through the courtesy of the Municipal Museum, Amsterdam. *Ill. p. 27.*

* 13 Paris through the Window. 1913 (dated). Oil on canvas, 52¼ x 54¾". Lent by the Solomon R. Guggenheim Foundation, New York. *Ill. p. 28.*

14 Musician. 1912-13 (dated). Oil on canvas, 74 x 62½". Lent by P. A. Regnault, through the courtesy of the Municipal Museum, Amsterdam.

15 Paris Self-Portrait with Seven Fingers. 1912-13. Oil on canvas, 49⅜ x 42¼". Lent by P. A. Regnault, through the courtesy of the Municipal Museum, Amsterdam.

16 The Drunkard (Interior). 1912-13 (dated). Oil on canvas, 33⅛ x 45⅛". Lent by Hjalmar Gabrielson, Gothenburg, Sweden.

* 17 Burning House. 1913 (dated). Oil on canvas, 42 x 47¼". Lent by Frau Nell Urech-Walden, Schinznach-Bad, Switzerland. *Ill. p. 30.*

* 18 The Praying Jew (The Rabbi of Vitebsk). 1914. Oil on canvas, 46 x 35". Lent by the Art Institute of Chicago, The Joseph Winterbotham Collection. *Ill. p. 35.*

19 Lisa. 1914. Oil on canvas, 31 x 18⅛". Lent by the artist.

* 20 Self-Portrait with Wineglass (Double Portrait). 1917. Oil on canvas, 92½ x 54". Lent by the Pierre Matisse Gallery, New York. *Ill. p. 41.*

21 Homage to Gogol. 1917. (Design for theatre curtain.) Watercolor, 15½ x 19¾". The Museum of Modern Art. Acquired through the Lillie P. Bliss Bequest.

* 22 The Market Place. c. 1917. Oil on canvas, 26 x 38¼". Lent anonymously, through the courtesy of the Worcester Museum. *Ill. p. 40.*

* 23 Cemetery. 1917 (dated). Oil on canvas, 27¼ x 39½". Lent by the artist. *Ill. p. 42.*

24 Gate to the Cemetery. 1917 (dated). Oil on canvas, 34¾ x 27¼". Lent by the artist.

* 25 The Green Violinist. 1918. Oil on canvas, 77 x 42½". Lent by the Solomon R. Guggenheim Foundation, New York. *Ill. p. 43.*

* 26 Blue House. 1920 (dated). Oil on canvas, 26⅛ x 38¼". Lent by the Museum of Fine Arts, Liège, Belgium. *Ill. p. 50.*

27 ENVIRONS OF VITEBSK. 1922. Oil on canvas, 28¾ x 36⅛". Lent by the artist. (Variant of a 1914 canvas of same title, now Collection Charles Im Obersteg, Basel, Switzerland.)

* 28 THE BIRTHDAY. 1915-23. Oil on canvas, 31⅞ x 39⅜". Lent by the Solomon R. Guggenheim Foundation, New York. *Ill. p. 37.*

29 GIRL BEFORE THE WINDOW. 1924. Oil on canvas, 41 x 39⅝". Lent by P. A. Regnault, through the courtesy of the Municipal Museum, Amsterdam.

* 30 DOUBLE PORTRAIT. 1924 (dated). Oil on canvas, 51¼ x 37⅜". Lent by Philippe Dotremont, Uccle-Brussels, Belgium. *Ill. p. 52.*

* 31 THE TROUGH. 1925. Oil on canvas, 57⅝ x 45⅛". Lent by the Vicomte de Noailles, Paris. *Ill. p. 55.*

* 32 THE CIRCUS. 1926 (dated). Oil on canvas, 46 x 35". Lent by Dr. Potvin, Brussels. *Ill. p. 57.*

33 THE MILLER, HIS SON AND THE ASS. For *The Fables of La Fontaine.* 1926 (dated). Gouache, 20 x 16". Lent by Mme Helena Rubinstein, New York.

34 CIRCUS RIDER. 1927. Gouache, 25 x 19". Lent by Mme Helena Rubinstein, New York.

35 THE BRIDE WITH THE DOUBLE FACE. 1927 (dated). Oil on canvas, 39⅜ x 28¾". Lent by the Pierre Matisse Gallery, New York.

36 HOMAGE TO THE EIFFEL TOWER. 1928. Oil on canvas, 35⅛ x 45⅞". Lent by Mlle Marcelle Berr de Turique, Neuilly-sur-Seine.

* 37 IN THE MOUNTAIN. 1930 (dated). Oil on canvas, 28 x 23". Lent by Mr. and Mrs. Joseph Bissett, New York. *Ill. p. 58.*

38 THE CREATION. 1930 (dated). Gouache, 25 x 18¾". Lent by the artist.

39 THE SACRIFICE OF ABRAHAM. 1931 (dated). Gouache and oil on paper, 26¼ x 20¼". Lent by the artist.

* 40 THE LOVERS IN THE FLOWERS (LILACS). 1931. Oil on canvas, 51 x 35". Lent by Josef von Sternberg, Hollywood. *Ill. p. 59.*

41 THE SACRIFICE OF NOAH. 1932 (dated). Gouache, 24½ x 19⅛". Lent by the artist.

42 THE WAILING WALL. Jerusalem, 1932 (dated). Oil on canvas, 29 x 36½". Lent by the artist.

* 43 SOLITUDE. 1933 (dated). Oil on canvas, 43⅝ x 66". Lent by the artist. *Ill. p. 60.*

44 NUDE OVER VITEBSK. 1933 (dated). Oil on canvas, 34⅞ x 45¾". Lent by the artist.

45 PORTRAIT OF THE ARTIST'S WIFE. 1934-35. Oil on canvas, 39⅜ x 32". Lent by P. A. Regnault, through the courtesy of the Municipal Museum, Amsterdam.

* 46 WHITE CRUCIFIXION. 1938. Oil on canvas, 61 x 55". Lent by the artist. *Ill. p. 62.*

* 47 THE CELLO PLAYER. 1939 (dated). Oil on canvas, 39½ x 28¾". Lent by P. A. Regnault, through the courtesy of the Municipal Museum, Amsterdam. *Ill. p. 67.*

* 48 THE BRIDE AND GROOM OF THE EIFFEL TOWER. 1938-39 (dated). Oil on canvas, 58¾ x 54⅛". Lent by the Pierre Matisse Gallery, New York. *Ill. p. 68.*

* 49 TIME IS A RIVER WITHOUT BANKS. 1930-39. Oil on canvas, 39⅜ x 32". The Museum of Modern Art. Given anonymously. *Ill. p. 65.*

50 SNOWING (LE NEIGE). 1939. Gouache and pastel, 25½ x 19½". Lent by the City Art Museum of St. Louis.

* 51 THE RED COCK. 1940 (dated). Oil on canvas, 29 x 36". Lent by Miss Mary E. Johnston, Glendale, Ohio. *Ill. p. 64.*

52 THE MADONNA OF THE VILLAGE. 1938-42 (dated). Oil on canvas, 38 x 36". Lent by Adolphe A. Juviler, New York.

53 THE JUGGLER. 1943 (dated). Oil on canvas, 43½ x 31". Lent by Mrs. Charles B. Goodspeed, Chicago.

54 IN THE NIGHT. 1943. Oil on canvas, 18¼ x 20¼". Lent by Louis E. Stern, New York.

55 BETWEEN DARKNESS AND LIGHT. 1943. Oil on canvas, 39¼ x 28¾". Lent by the Pierre Matisse Gallery, New York.

56 RED HORSE AND LOVERS. 1938-1944 (dated). Oil on canvas, 45⅛ x 40⅛". Lent by the artist.

57 THE RED COCK IN THE NIGHT. 1944. Oil on canvas, 26¾ x 31". Lent by John S. Newberry, Jr., Grosse Pointe Farms, Michigan.

* 58 LISTENING TO THE COCK. 1944. Oil on canvas, 38½ x 28". Lent by Adolphe A. Juviler, New York. *Ill. p. 69.*

59 HOUSE WITH EYE. 1945. Oil on canvas, 23⅛ x 20⅛". Lent by Miss Ida Gordey, New York.

* 60 SPIRIT OF THE TOWN. 1945 (dated). Oil on canvas, 42 x 32". Lent by the Pierre Matisse Gallery, New York. *Ill. p. 70.*

61 MORNING REVEILLE. 1945 (dated). Oil on canvas, 39⅞ x 33". Lent by Mr. and Mrs. Walter Paepcke, Chicago.

Prints

All dimensions describe plate size. Unless otherwise noted all prints have been lent by the artist.

MEIN LEBEN. Berlin, 1923

Series of 20 plates illustrating the artist's autobiography. Issued in album form without text by Paul Cassirer. *In this listing titles are followed by the original album number.*

* 63 THE GRANDFATHERS. (#3) Drypoint, 10⅞ x 8 7/16". *Ill. p. 77.*

64 HOUSE IN VITEBSK. (#11) "La Calèche Volante" inscribed in pencil. Drypoint with watercolor, 9⅞ x 7⅜". Lent by the Solomon R. Guggenheim Foundation.

65 GRANDFATHER'S HOUSE. (#12) Drypoint, 6 5/16 x 8½".

66 THE FATHER'S TOMB. (#20) "La Tombe, 1914" inscribed in pencil. Drypoint and etching with watercolor, 4¼ x 5⅞". Lent by the Solomon R. Guggenheim Foundation.

INDEPENDENT PRINTS

* 67 ACROBAT WITH VIOLIN. Paris, 1924. Etching and drypoint with watercolor (trial proof), 16⅜ x 12½". *Ill. p. 73.*

68 SELF-PORTRAIT WITH GRIMACE. Paris, 1924-25. Etching with aquatint, 16⅜ x 12½".

DEAD SOULS. Paris, 1923-27

Novel by Nikolai V. Gogol, illustrated by 96 etchings, as well as vignettes and historiated initial letters. Commissioned by Ambroise Vollard. Unpublished. *In this listing the plate number following the title refers to the Vollard edition.*

69 THE DEPARTURE OF CHITCHIKOV. (Pl. 9) Etching and drypoint, 11¼ x 8⅝".

* 70 MME KOROBOTCHKA. (Pl. 15) Etching and drypoint, 11¾ x 8⅞". *Ill. p. 78.*

* 71 THE BARN YARD. (Pl. 17) Etching and drypoint, 9 x 11 9/16". *Ill. p. 78.*

72 WELCOME TO CHITCHIKOV. (Pl. 20) Etching and drypoint, 11 x 9⅛".

73 SOBAKEVITCH. (Pl. 33) Etching and drypoint, 10⅞ x 8¼".

74 MME SOBAKEVITCH. (Pl. 34) Etching and drypoint, 10⅞ x 8⅜".

* 75 CHITCHIKOV AND SOBAKEVITCH. (Pl. 38) Etching and drypoint, 8⅜ x 10⅞". *Ill. p. 79.*

76 LANDSCAPE. (Pl. 42) Etching and drypoint, 11 x 8½".

77 INTERIOR. (Pl. 49) Etching and drypoint, 11 x 8½".

* 78 CHANCELLERY. (Pl. 64) Etching and drypoint, 11 x 8¾". *Ill. p. 79.*

THE FABLES. PARIS, 1927-31

Poems by Jean de la Fontaine, illustrated by 100 etchings. Commissioned by Ambroise Vollard. Unpublished. *In this listing numerals following the title refer to the number of the book and poem under which the fable may be found in any standard edition of the text.*

* 79 THE TWO GOATS. (XII:14) Etching and drypoint, 11⅝ x 9 5/16". *Ill. p. 81.*

80 THE EAGLE AND THE BEETLE. (II:18) Etching and drypoint, 11⅝ x 9⅜".

81 THE SUN AND THE FROGS. (XI:10; or VI:12) Etching and drypoint, 11 7/16 x 9⅜".

82 THE CROW WHO WISHED TO IMITATE THE EAGLE. (II:16) Etching and drypoint, 11⅝ x 9 7/16".

83 THE JAY DRESSED IN PEACOCK FEATHERS. (IV:9) Etching and drypoint, 11⅜ x 9¼".

84 THE WOLF AND THE STORK. (III:9) Etching and drypoint, 11½ x 9 5/16".

85 THE FUNERAL OF THE LIONESS. (VIII:14) Etching and drypoint, 11⅝ x 9⅜".

86 THE FOX WITH THE CROPPED TAIL. (V:5) Etching and drypoint, 11½ x 9⅞".

87 THE TWO PIGEONS. (IX:2) Etching and drypoint, 11⅝ x 9⅜".

* 88 THE ASS LOADED WITH SALT AND THE ASS LOADED WITH SPONGES. (II:10) Etching and drypoint, 11¾ x 9 9/16". *Ill. p. 81.*

* 89 THE LARK AND THE FARMER. (IV:22) Etching and drypoint, 11⅝ x 9½". *Ill. p. 82.*

* 90 THE FOX AND THE GRAPES. (III:11) Etching and drypoint, 11½ x 9 7/16". *Ill. p. 80.*

91 THE TWO PARROTS, THE KING AND HIS SON. (X:11) Etching and drypoint, 11⅝ x 9⅜".

* 92 THE CAT METAMORPHOSED INTO A WOMAN. (II:18) Etching and drypoint, 11⅝ x 9½". *Ill. p. 80.*

THE BIBLE. Paris, 1929-39

Illustrations commissioned by Ambroise Vollard. At the time of Vollard's death 105 plates, or more than half of the series, had been completed. In the projected edition extracts from the biblical text were to serve as titles for the plates. *Titles listed below are identification titles.*

93 THE APPARITION OF THE RAINBOW TO NOAH. Etching and drypoint, 12 x 9".

* 94 THE APPARITION OF THE ANGEL TO JOSHUA. Etching and drypoint, 11¾ x 9¼". *Ill. p. 75.*

* 95 UNTITLED (for one of the books of the Prophets). Etching and drypoint, 13⅝ x 10⅞". *Ill. p. 85.*

* 96 ABRAHAM MOURNS SARAH. Etching and drypoint, 11½ x 9½". *Ill. p. 83.*

97 PROPHET KILLED BY A LION. Etching and drypoint, 12⅝ x 8⅝".

* 98 JACOB'S DREAM. Etching and drypoint, 11⅝ x 9⅝". *Ill. p. 83.*

100 THE SACRIFICE OF ABRAHAM. Etching and drypoint, 12 x 9⅜".

101 KING DAVID PLAYING HIS HARP. Etching and drypoint, 12½ x 9⅜".

102 THE SACRIFICE OF NOAH. Etching and drypoint, 11¹³⁄₁₆ x 9⁷⁄₁₆".

103 THE VISION OF THE PROPHET ELIJAH. Etching and drypoint, 12½ x 7⅞".

* 104 DAVID WITH THE HEAD OF GOLIATH. Etching and drypoint, 11⅛ x 9½". *Ill. p. 84.*

* 105 ABRAHAM APPROACHING SODOM WITH THREE ANGELS. Etching, 12¹⁄₁₆ x 9⁵⁄₁₆". *Ill. p. 86.*

Theatre Designs

106 Preparatory drawing with watercolor for mural in State Jewish Theatre, Moscow. 1919. Lent by the artist.

* 107 Stage set for *Congratulations.* 1919. Lent by the artist. *Ill. p. 48.*

108-113 Costume designs for *Congratulations*, *That's a Lie* and *The Police.* 1919. Lent by the artist.

114-129 Four curtain designs, 10 costume designs and 2 choreographic sketches for the ballet *Aleko.* 1942. The Museum of Modern Art, Dance and Theatre Design Collection.

130-144 Four curtain designs, 10 costume designs for the ballet, *Firebird.* 1945. Lent by the artist.

ONE-MAN EXHIBITIONS

1914 BERLIN. *Der Sturm* gallery.

1921 MOSCOW. *State Jewish Theatre* (auditorium).

1923 BERLIN. *Galerie Lutz.*

1924 BRUSSELS. *Galerie du Centaure.* March 22–April 2.
PARIS. *Galerie Barbazanges-Hodebert.* Dec. 17–30. (Retrospective)

1925 COLOGNE. *Kölnischer Kunstverein.* April.
DRESDEN. *Galerie Ernst Arnold.* Aug.–Dec.
PARIS. *Aux Quatre Chemins.* Oct. 27–Nov. 10.

1926 NEW YORK. *Reinhardt Galleries.* Jan. 9–30. (Retrospective)
CHICAGO. *The Arts Club of Chicago.* March.
PARIS. *Galerie Granoff.* June 14–July 5.
PARIS. *Galerie Granoff.* Nov. 22–Dec. 11.

1928 PARIS. *Galerie Le Portique.* March 10–17.

1929 COLOGNE. *Kunstgewerbe Museum.*
BRUSSELS. *Galerie L'Epoque.* March.

1930 PARIS. *Galerie Bernheim-Jeune.* Feb. 10–21.
BRUSSELS. *Le Centaure.* March 1–19.
BERLIN. *Galerie Flechtheim.* April.
The three exhibitions above consisted of gouaches for the *Fables* of La Fontaine.
NEW YORK. *Demotte Gallery.* Nov. 10–Dec. 6.

1931 SAN FRANCISCO. *California Palace of the Legion of Honor.* March–April.
PARIS. *Galerie Le Portique.* June 13–30.

1932 AMSTERDAM. *Society of Dutch Artists.*

1933 THE HAGUE. *Esher Surrey Gallery.*
BASEL. *Kunsthalle.* Nov. 4–Dec. 3. (Retrospective)

1934 PRAGUE. *Dra Feigla Gallery.*

1935 LONDON. *Leicester Galleries.* April–May.

1936 NEW YORK. *New Art Circle.* (J. B. Neumann) Nov. 30–Dec. 31.

1938 BRUSSELS. *Palais des Beaux Arts.* Feb. 22–March 13.
NEW YORK. *Lilienfeld Galleries.* Feb. 28–March 26.

1939 NEW YORK. *Lilienfeld Galleries*. Dec. 5–Jan. 7.

1940 PARIS. *Galerie Mai*. Jan. 26–Feb. 24.

1941 NEW YORK. *Pierre Matisse Gallery*. Nov. 25–Dec. 13.

1942 NEW YORK. *Pierre Matisse Gallery*. Oct. 13–Nov. 7.

1943 NEW YORK. *Pierre Matisse Gallery*. Nov. 2–27.

1944 NEW YORK. *Pierre Matisse Gallery*. Oct. 31–Nov. 30.

1945 CHICAGO. *The Arts Club*. Jan.
BOSTON. *Institute of Modern Art*. Jan. 24–Feb. 25 (with Soutine).
LOS ANGELES. *James Vigeveno Galleries*. April 1–30.
NEW YORK. *Pierre Matisse Gallery*. June 5–23.

1946 NEW YORK. *Pierre Matisse Gallery*. Feb. 5–March 2.

1946 NEW YORK. *The Museum of Modern Art*. April 9–June 23.
CHICAGO. *The Art Institute*. Oct. 24–Dec. 15.

WORKS BY CHAGALL IN AMERICAN PUBLIC COLLECTIONS

BALTIMORE, MD. The Baltimore Museum of Art
1 gouache (on extended loan)

BROOKLYN, N. Y. The Brooklyn Museum
2 prints

BUFFALO, N. Y. Albright Art Gallery
2 oils
1 gouache

CAMBRIDGE, MASS. Fogg Museum of Art
3 prints

CHICAGO, Ill. The Art Institute of Chicago
1 oil
1 gouache
1 print

DETROIT, MICH. Detroit Institute of Art
1 oil

LOS ANGELES, CALIF. Los Angeles Museum of History, Science and Art
3 gouaches

NEW HAVEN, CONN. Yale University (*Société Anonyme* Collection)
2 prints

NEW YORK, N. Y. Art of This Century
1 oil

NEW YORK, N. Y. The Museum of Modern Art
2 oils
2 gouaches
1 watercolor
3 prints
67 ballet costume and decor designs

NEW YORK, N. Y. New York Public Library. Print Room
3 prints

NEW YORK, N. Y. Solomon R. Guggenheim Foundation
10 oils
10 watercolors
1 gouache
1 drawing
2 etchings with watercolor

NORTHAMPTON, MASS. Smith College
1 gouache

PHILADELPHIA, Pa. Philadelphia Museum of Art
1 drawing
3 prints

SAN FRANCISCO, CALIF. San Francisco Museum of Art
1 watercolor

ST. LOUIS, MO. City Art Museum of St. Louis
1 gouache

ST. LOUIS, MO. Washington University
1 print

WASHINGTON, D. C. Phillips Memorial Gallery
1 oil
1 pastel

WORCESTER, MASS. Worcester Art Museum
2 oils
2 watercolors
3 gouaches
(Extended loans)

ILLUSTRATED BOOKS

Only published books are listed below. Chagall's most important book illustrations, Gogol's *Dead Souls*, *The Fables of La Fontaine* and the Bible, all commissioned by Ambroise Vollard, are still unpublished. For information concerning them see pages 89-90 in the catalog of the exhibition.

1914 Niestor. *Tales*. Wilna, Klezkine.
Reproductions of 9 drawings.

1915 Peretz. *The Magician*. Wilna, Klezkine.
Reproductions of 3 drawings.

1920 Philippe Soupault. *Rose des Vents*. Paris, Au Sans Pareil.
Reproductions of 4 drawings.

1922 D. Hofstein. *Trauer*. Moscow, Kulturliege.
Reproductions of 6 drawings.

1925 Claire and Ivan Goll. *Poèmes d'Amour*. Paris, Budry.
Reproductions of 4 drawings.

1925 Claire Goll. *Journal d'un cheval*. Paris, Budry.
Reproductions of 4 drawings.

1926 Jean Giraudoux, Paul Morand, Pierre Mac Orlan, André Salmon, Max Jacob, Jacques de Lacretelle, Joseph Kessel. *Les Sept Péchés Capitaux*. Paris, Simon Kra.
15 etchings.

1926 Marcel Arland. *Maternité*. Paris, Au Sans Pareil.
5 etchings.

1926 Gustave Coquiot. *En suivant la Seine*. Paris, Delpeuch.
Reproductions of drawings.

1926 François Lehel. *Notre Art dément*. Paris, H. Jonquières et Cie.
Limited edition contains one etching.

1927 Gustave Coquiot. *Suite provinciale*. Paris, Delpeuch.
Reproductions of 92 drawings.

1927 Paul Morand. *Ouvert la nuit*. Paris, N.R.F.
One portrait drawing of the author reproduced.

1927 Marcel Arland. *Etapes*. Paris, N.R.F.
One portrait drawing of the author reproduced.

1928 Ilarie Voronca. *Ulise*. Budapest, Colectuinen interglad.
One portrait drawing of the author reproduced.

1929 René Schwob. *Une Mélodie silencieuse*. Paris, Grasset.
Reproduction of one drawing.

1931 René Schwob. *Marc Chagall et l'Ame juive*. Paris, R. A. Correa.
Limited edition contains 2 etchings.

1931 Marc Chagall. *Ma Vie*. Paris, Stock.
Reproductions of 32 drawings.

1933 Joseph Opatoshu. *Ein Tag in Regensberg*. New York, Malino.
One drawing reproduced.

1938 Abraham Walt. *Songs and Poems, 1888-1938*. New York, Forward Association.
Reproductions of 32 drawings.

1943 Raïssa Maritain. *Marc Chagall*. New York, Editions de la Maison Française.
One drawing reproduced.

1944 Itzik Feffer. *Heinland*. New York, Icor Association.
Reproductions of 8 drawings.

1945 Bella Chagall. *Brenendicke Licht*. New York, Book League of the Jewish Peoples Fraternal Order.
Reproductions of 25 drawings.

1946 Bella Chagall. *Burning Lights*. New York, Shocken Books Inc.
Reproductions of 36 drawings.

1946 Claire Goll. *Diary of a Horse*. Brooklyn, Editions Hémisphères.
Reproductions of 4 drawings.

n.d. Pierre Reverdy. *Pierres Blanches*. Carcassonne.
One drawing reproduced.

THEATRE DESIGNS

1917 Curtain designs for three plays by Gogol: *Marriage*, *The Cardplayers*, *The Departure*. Stage set and costume designs for *Marriage*. Hermitage Theatre, Petrograd. *Unexecuted*.

1919 Stage sets and costumes for three one-act plays by Sholom Aleichem: *Congratulations*, *The Police*, *That's a Lie*. State Jewish Theatre (GOSET), Moscow. *Produced by Granovsky*, 1921.

1920 Stage sets and costume designs for Gogol's *Revizor*. Theatre for Revolutionary Satire (TEREWSAT), Moscow. *Not produced*.

1921 Stage sets and costume designs for John Synge's *Playboy of the Western World*. Second Moscow Art Theatre. *Unexecuted*.

1942 Scenery and costumes for the ballet, *Aleko*. Book from Pushkin's poem *The Gypsies;* music, Tchaikovsky's Piano Trio; choreography, Leonide Massine. *Produced by The Ballet Theatre*.

1945 Scenery and costumes for the ballet, *Firebird*. Book from the Russian fairy tale; music by Igor Stravinsky; choreography, Adolph Bolm; artistic collaboration, Henry Clifford. *Produced by The Ballet Theatre*.

BIBLIOGRAPHY

In the compilation of this bibliography, the artist's scrapbooks as well as all known published lists of works on Chagall (see especially bibl.91,116,181) have been consulted. Not included here are references to exhibition notices which have appeared in American newspapers, and to most exhibition notices listed in Art Index, 1929-1945. Also omitted are a few references to material in foreign journals mentioned in bibl.91,116,181 which could not be verified by the compiler, and to some information in the artist's scrapbooks and elsewhere which was considered of lesser importance.

The arrangement is alphabetical, under the author's name, or under the title in the case of unsigned articles and collective works. Publications of museums are entered under the name of the institution when that name is distinctive; otherwise, under the name of the city in which it is located. Exhibition catalogs issued by private galleries and art organizations are listed under the name of the gallery or group. All material except items preceded by † has been examined by the compiler.

ABBREVIATIONS. Ag August, Ap April, Aufl Auflage, Bd Band, col colored, D December, ed editor(s), edited, edition, F February, hft Heft, il illustration(s), Ja January, Je June, Jy July, Mr March, My May, N November, n.d. not dated, no number, ns new series, p page(s), por portrait(s), S September, ser series.

SAMPLE ENTRY for magazine article. CASSOU, JEAN. Marc Chagall. il Art et Décoration 34:65-76 S 1930.

EXPLANATION. An article by Jean Cassou, entitled "Marc Chagall," accompanied by illustrations will be found in *Art et Décoration*, volume 34, pages 65-76 inclusive, the September 1930 issue.

* Items so marked are in the Museum Library.

HANNAH B. MULLER

Writings by Chagall

1 CE QUE PENSENT LES PEINTRES DE L'EXPOSITION D'ART ITALIEN. Bête Noire (Paris) O 1 1935.

2 CHAGALL . . . RÉPOND À L'ENQUÊTE DE BEAUX ARTS SUR LE MÉTIER. Beaux-Arts (Paris) ns74no196:1 O 2 1936.

3 DELACROIX ET NOS PEINTRES. L'Intransigeant (Paris) Je 9 1930.

4 IN MEMORY OF M. M. VINAVER. Razsviet (Paris) p11 O 24 1926.
Russian text. Also appeared in Zveno p23 O 24 1926.

* 5 MA VIE. Préface d'André Salmon. 253p il Paris, Stock, 1931.
Published in Yiddish in Die Zukunft (New York) 30:158-62, 211-14, 290-3, 407-10 Mr-Je 1925. Translated into Hebrew by Manasseh Levin 94p il Tel Aviv, "Sifriat Poalim" Workers' Book-Guild (Hashomer Hatzair), 1943. Excerpts published in
* Westheim, Paul, ed. Künstlerbekenntnisse. p159-63 il Berlin, Propyläen Verlag, n.d.; in
* View (New York) ser5no6:7,12,14 Ja 1946,
* in Commentary (New York) 1no6:30-3 Ap 1946; in Russian, in Razsviet (Paris) p6-7 My 4 1930, and in bibl.116.

———See also 167.

* 6 MESSAGE DE MARC CHAGALL AUX PEINTRES FRANÇAIS. Spectateur des Arts (Paris) no1:3 D 1944.

7 MODERN ART. Moznayim (Tel Aviv) 2no46-7:14-15; no48:12-13 Mr-Ap 1931.
Hebrew text.

8 MY FIRST TEACHERS: PEN. il Razsviet (Paris) Ja 30 1927.
Russian text.

9 QUELQUES IMPRESSIONS SUR LA PEINTURE FRANÇAISE. Renaissance (École Libre des Hautes Études, New York) 2-3:45-57 1944-5.

10 [RÉPONSE À] NOTRE ENQUÊTE SUR LA CRISE DE LA PEINTURE. por Beaux Arts (Brussels) Ag 19 1935.

* 11 [RÉPONSE À UNE] ENQUÊTE: POUVEZ-VOUS DIRE QUELLE A ÉTÉ LA RENCONTRE CAPITALE DE VOTRE VIE. Minotaure no3-4: 106 1933.

* 12 [RÉPONSE À UNE ENQUÊTE SUR L'ART D'AUJOURD'HUI] il Cahiers d'Art 10no1-4:37, 39-44 1935.

13 Voyage en Hollande. L'Intransigeant (Paris) My 3 1932.

14 Voyage en Palestine. L'Intransigeant (Paris) Je 8 1931.

SEE ALSO 44, 54, 65, 70, 84, 85, 92, 125, 141, 143, 151, 168, 170

Poems Dedicated to Chagall

* 15 Apollinaire, Guillaume. Rotsoge. Au peintre Chagall. Cahiers d'Art 14no5-10:150 1939.
Written on the occasion of the Chagall exhibition at "Der Sturm" Gallery, Berlin, 1914. Published with variations under title: *A Travers l'Europe* in the author's Calligrammes, Paris, Mercure de France, 1918. Also published in bibl.116, p54.

16 Audiberti. Marc Chagall. Nouvelle Revue Française 28:714-15 My 1 1940.

17 Cendrars, Blaise. Portrait; Atelier. *In* the author's Dix-neuf poèmes élastiques. p12-16 Paris, Au Sans Pareil, 1919.
Poems dated October 1913. Reprinted in bibl.116, p55-7. *Portrait*, first published in Der Sturm, Jy 1918, is translated into * German in Walden, Herwarth, ed. Expressionismus. p20 Berlin, Verlag Der Sturm, 1918, and in bibl.115.

* 18 Fierens, Paul. Visite à Chagall. *In* Marc Chagall. p3 Anvers, Éditions Sélection, 1929. (Sélection: chronique de la vie artistique. 6)

* 19 Maritain, Raïssa. Chagall. *In* the author's Marc Chagall. p9-11 New York, Éditions de la Maison Française, 1943.

† 20 Salmon, André. Parabole des comédiens en voyage. *In* the author's Métamorphoses de la harpe et de la harpiste, 1926.
Reprinted in bibl.116, p57-8.

Books, Articles, Catalogs

21 Alberti, Rafael. Paris—Chagall. El Sol Ag 2 1931.

Amberg, George. See 117.

22 Aranovitch, G. The artists of Paris: Marc Chagall. il Krasnaia Panorama (Moscow) no47:13 N 23 1928.
Russian text.

* 23 Aronson, Boris. Marc Chagall. 30p plus 21 plates(1 col) Berlin, Razum Verlag, 1924.
First published in Russian in 1923 by Petropolis-Verlag.

24 Arts Club of Chicago. Marc Chagall. 2p il [1945]
Exhibition catalog listing 39 works.

25 Barbazanges-Hodebert, Galerie, Paris. Oeuvres de Marc Chagall de 1908 à 1924. 6p 1924.
Exhibition catalog listing 115 works.

26 Barchan, Pawel. Marc Chagall. il Deutsche Kunst und Dekoration 59:292-9 F 1927.

27 Barotte, René. Marc Chagall. Homme Libre (Paris) Je 29 1931.
Exhibition, Galerie Le Portique, Paris.

Barr, Alfred H., Jr. See 129.

* 28 Basel. Kunsthalle. Marc Chagall. 19p plus 8 plates 1933.
Exhibition catalog listing 172 works. Introduction by Gilles de la Tourette.

Bazin, Germain. See 91.

29 "Beaux-arts" et "La Gazette des Beaux-arts," Paris. Peintres instinctifs: naissance de l'expressionisme. p[8-9,11-13] 1936.
Exhibition catalog listing 35 works. Catalog by Raymond Cogniat; introduction by André Salmon.

30 Benois, Alexander. Chagall exhibition. Posledniia Novosti (Paris) F 3 1940.
Russian text. Exhibition, Galerie Mai, Paris. Part, translated into French, in Cahiers d'Art 15no1-2:33 1940.

31 ———Exhibition of the instinctualists. Posledniia Novosti (Paris) Ja 4 1936.
Russian text. Exhibition, Beaux-Arts Gallery, Paris.

32 ———The return to subject matter. Posledniia Novosti (Paris) Ja 20 1934.
Russian text.

33 Bernheim-Jeune, Galerie, Paris. La Fontaine par Chagall. 14p il 1930.
Exhibition catalog with introduction by Ambroise Vollard reprinted from L'Intransigeant Ja 14 1929 (bibl.185). Similar catalogs published by Galerie Le Centaure, Paris, 8p il 1930, and by Galerie Flechtheim, Berlin, 16p il 1930.

34 BIELINKY, J. Marc Chagall à l'exposition d'art sacré moderne. il Terre Retrouvée (Paris) 11no6:5 D 15 1938.
Criticism of Chagall's etchings for the Bible.

34a BILLE, EJLER. Picasso, surrealisme, abstrakt kunst. p102-12 il (1 col) por Copenhagen, Forlaget Helios, 1945.

* 35 BRETON, ANDRÉ. Le surréalisme et la peinture, suivi de Genèse et perspective artistique du surréalisme. p89 il New York, Brentano's, 1945.
Text dated 1941. Published in English in
* Guggenheim, Peggy, ed. Art of this century. p19 New York, Art of This Century, 1942.

BRINTON, CHRISTIAN. See 144.

36 BRUSSELS. PALAIS DES BEAUX ARTS. Marc Chagall. 11p il 1938.
Exhibition catalog listing 62 works.

* 37 BULLIET, CLARENCE JOSEPH. Apples & madonnas. p155-6 il Chicago, Covici, 1927.

* 38 ———The significant moderns and their pictures. p77-80 il New York, Covici Friede, 1936.

39 CANUDO. Chagall. Paris Journal Jy 11 1914.

* 40 CASSOU, JEAN. Marc Chagall. il Art et Décoration 34:65-76 S 1930.

41 LE CENTAURE, GALERIE, PARIS. Oeuvres de Marc Chagall. 4p 1924.
Exhibition catalog listing 50 works.

———See also 33.

* 42 CHAGALL. Current Biography 1943:115-17.

43 CHAPMAN, MANUEL. On certain aspects of Chagall's art. il Chicago Evening Post Magazine of the Art World Mr 16 1926.

44 CHARENSOL, GEORGES. Chez Marc Chagall. il Paris Journal My 16 1924.
Interview with Chagall.

———See also 116.

* 45 CHENEY, SHELDON. A primer of modern art. 10th ed. p206-7 New York, Tudor Publishing Co., 1939.

46 COGNIAT, RAYMOND. Visite d'atelier. il por Beaux-Arts (Paris) ns73no56:3 Ja 26 1934.

———See also 29.

47 COLLEYE, HUBERT. La Fontaine vu par Chagall. il Metropole (Antwerp) Mr 9 1930.

48 COQUIOT, GUSTAVE. Cubistes, futuristes, passéistes. [Nouvelle éd.] p9-11 il Paris, Ollendorff, 1923.
Not included in earlier editions of the same work.

* 49 ———Les indépendants, 1884-1920. 4e éd. p57-60 il Paris, Ollendorff [1920?]

50 ———Vagabondages. p262-7 Paris, Ollendorff, 1921.

———See also 116.

51 CORNETTE, A. Marc Chagall. il Beaux Arts (Brussels) Ap 10 1931.
Reprint of excerpts from catalog published in connection with Salon de l'Art Contemporain in Antwerp.

* 52 COURTHION, PIERRE. Chagall et les "Fables." il Cahiers d'Art 4no5:215-21 1929.

53 ———Marc Chagall. Revue Hebdomadaire (Paris) 4:107-9 Ap 1928.

54 ———Marc Chagall. por Nouvelles Littéraires (Paris) p7 Ap 30 1932.
Interview with Chagall.

———See also 116.

* 55 DÄUBLER, THEODOR. Chagall. il Der Cicerone 12hft4:139-49 F 1920.
Reprinted in Jahrbuch der Jungen Kunst 1920:57-67.

56 ———Marc Chagall. 13p plus 32 plates Rome, Éditions de "Valori Plastici," 1922.

DELTEIL, JOSEPH. See 116.

* 57 DEMOTTE, NEW YORK. Paintings by Marc Chagall. 7p por 1930.
Exhibition catalog listing 27 works. Includes bibliography.

58 DREYFUS, ALBERT. Der Maler Marc Chagall. il Deutsche Kunst und Dekoration 67:356-70 Mr 1931.

58a Du Colombier, Pierre. La Fontaine et Chagall. Candide (Paris) 7no310:6 F 20 1930.

* 59 ———& Manuel, Roland. Les arts. p114 Paris, Denoël et Steele, 1933. (Tableau du XXe siècle 1900-1933)

Edouard-Joseph. See 74.

60 Eeckhout, Door van den. Marc Chagall's illustraties bij Fabels van La Fontaine. il Elsevier's Geïllustreerd Maandschrift (Amsterdam) 80:159-65 S 1930.

Efross, A. See 116.

* 61 ——— & Tugendhold, Ia. Die Kunst Marc Chagalls. 77p il por Potsdam, Kiepenheuer, 1921.
First published in Russian 51p plus 13 plates(1 col) Moscow, "Gelikon," 1918. Excerpts are reprinted in Das Kunstblatt 5:1-9 1921.

* 62 Einstein, Carl. Die Kunst des 20. Jahr hunderts. 2. Aufl. p171-3, 483-93 il Berlin, Propyläen-Verlag, 1926. (Propyläen-Kunstgeschichte, XVI)

* 62a Engelman, Jan. Torso. p60-2 il Utrecht, De Gemeenschap, 1931.

63 Feigla, Galerie, Prague. Marc Chagall. 7p 1934.
Exhibition catalog listing 52 works.

64 Fels, Florent. Les expositions. Nouvelles Littéraires (Paris) p4 N 14 1925.
Exhibition, Galerie des Quatre Chemins, Paris.

* 65 ———Propos d'artistes. p29-34 por Paris, La Renaissance du Livre, 1925.
Includes statements by Chagall. Reprinted from Nouvelles Littéraires (Paris) Je 14 1924.

* 66 Fierens, Paul. Marc Chagall. 15p plus 32 plates Paris, Crès, 1929.
First published with variations, in Revue d'Art (Antwerp) 46:81-92 Mr 1929.

67 ———Marc Chagall, peintre du bonheur. il Beaux Arts (Brussels) p14-16, 28 Ja 14 1938.
Occasioned by exhibition of Chagall's work at Palais des Beaux-Arts, Brussels.

Flechtheim, Galerie, Berlin. See 33.

68 Fondane, Benjamin. Marc Chagall. il Chisla (Berlin) 1:189-91 1930.
Russian text.

69 ———Marc Chagall. il Cahiers Juifs (Paris) no9:266-72 Ap-My 1934.

70 Franklin, Harold. Marc Chagall, a wild beast of art. por Jewish Layman 7no2:3 O 1932.
Interview with Chagall.

71 G., K. Quelques mots sur Marc Chagall. Renaissance de l'Art Français 9:1043 D 1926.
Text in French and English.

* 72 Gagnon, Maurice. Peinture moderne. p170-1 il Montreal, Valiquette, 1940.
Criticism of *I and the Village* and *Jewish Wedding*.

73 George, Waldemar. A propos de l'exposition Chagall à la Galerie du Portique. Presse (Paris) Mr 20 1928.
For the most part a discussion of Chagall's illustrations for Gogol's *Les Ames Mortes*.

* 74 ———Chagall. *In* Edouard-Joseph. Dictionnaire biographique des artistes contemporains, 1910-1930. 1:262-7 il Paris, Art et Édition, 1930.

75 ———Chagall à Paris. il Sélection (Antwerp) ns 3e année 1:259-63 1923-4.

* 76 ———Marc Chagall. 63p il Paris, Éditions de la Nouvelle Revue Française, 1928. (Les Peintres français nouveaux, no31)
Includes bibliography.

77 ———Voici Chagall. il Paris Journal D 19 1924.
Exhibition, Galerie Barbazanges-Hodebert, Paris.

———See also 116.

77a Gilles De La Tourette, François. La peinture française contemporaine. p[9-10] il Paris, Librairie des Arts Décoratifs, 1937. (Les Maîtres de l'art indépendant)

———See also 28.

78 Girou, Jean. Le rêve coloré de Marc Chagall. il Aesculape (Paris) 22:113-15 Ap 1932.

* 79 ———Marc Chagall, citoyen de Limoux. *In* the author's Peintres du Midi. p133-9 il Paris, Floury, n.d.
Also published in Sud Magazine (Marseille) p16,18 Mr 16 1932.

GOLDWATER, ROBERT J. See 168.

* 80 GÓMEZ DE LA SERNA, RAMÓN. Pintura voladora. il Saber Vivir (Buenos Aires) 5no52: 22-4 D 1944.

81 GRANOFF, GALERIE, PARIS. Trente peintures de Marc Chagall. 4p il 1926.
Exhibition catalog listing 27 works.

82 ———Marc Chagall . . . travaux de l'été. 2p 1926.
Exhibition catalog listing 16 works.

83 GRUYTER, W. JOS. DE. Marc Chagall in den Kunsthandel Esther Surrey, Den Haag. il Elsevier's Geïllustreerd Maandschrift (Amsterdam) 83:290-4 Ap 1932.

84 GUENNE, JACQUES. Marc Chagall. il Art Vivant 3no72:999-1004, 1010-11 D 15 1927.
Includes interview with Chagall.

———See also 167.

* 85 GUGGENHEIM, PEGGY, ed. Art of this century. p46 il New York, Art of this century, 1942.
Includes statement by Chagall.

86 HAESAERTS, LUC. Marc Chagall. il Combat (Brussels) Ja 29 1938.
Occasioned by exhibition at Palais des Beaux-Arts, Brussels.

87 HALLE, FANINA W. Marc Chagall. il Das Kunstblatt 6:507-18 1922.

88 HAMMACHER, A. M. Marc Chagall. 8p plus 8 plates Amsterdam, "De Spieghel," Antwerpen, "Het Kompas" [1940]

89 HARLAIRE, ANDRÉ. Marc Chagall. Sélection (Antwerp) ns 4e année 1:360-2 1924-5.
Exhibition, Galerie Barbazanges-Hodebert, Paris.

* 90 HILDEBRANDT, HANS. Die Kunst des 19. und 20. Jahrhunderts. p419-21 il Wildpark-Potsdam, Akädemische Verlagsgesellschaft Athenaion, 1924.

* 91 HUYGHE, RENÉ. Histoire de l'art contemporain; la peinture. passim il por Paris, Alcan, 1935.
Includes bibliography; and essay by Germain Bazin, first published in Amour de l'Art 15:321-4 Mr 1934.

92 ISRAEL, MADELEINE. Exposition Chagall, Le "Portique." Univers Israélite (Paris) Jy 31 1931.
Includes statement by Chagall.

* 93 JEDLICKA, GOTTHARD. Begegnungen mit Künstlern der Gegenwart. 2. Aufl. p185-96 por Erlenbach-Zürich, E. Rentsch [1945]

* 94 JOHNSON, UNA E. Ambroise Vollard, éditeur. p71-4 il New York, Wittenborn, 1944.

* 95 KARPFEN, FRITZ. Gegenwartskunst: Russland. p25-8 il Wien, Verlag "Literaria," 1921.

* 96 KRAUS, FELIX. Marc Chagall, soñador. il Norte 3no1:26-7 N 1942.

97 KUHN, ALFRED. Der Fall Chagall. Anlässlich der ersten kollektiv-Ausstellung bei Lutz . . . in Berlin. Kunstchronik und Kunstmarkt 58no16:289-92 Ja 19 1923.

* 98 LANGUI, EM. Nieuw werk door Marc Chagall in de U.S.A. geschapen. il Zondagspost (Brussels) p8 il por N 4 1945.

* 99 LEICESTER GALLERIES, LONDON. Catalogue of an exhibition of paintings and gouaches by Marc Chagall. 11p 1935.
Exhibition catalog, listing 46 works, with foreword by R. H. Wilenski.

100 LEVINSON, ANDRÉ. Divagation au sujet d'une peinture de Chagall. il Renaissance de l'Art Français 10:133-41 Mr 1927.
English and French text. For the most part, criticism of *Les Amoureux* shown at Salon des Tuileries, 1925.

101 ———Chagall en Russie. il Amour de l'Art 4:727-32 O 1923.

102 LHOTE, ANDRÉ. Exposition Chagall. Nouvelle Revue Française 28:416-19 Mr 1 1940.
Exhibition, Galerie Mai, Paris.

103 ———Exposition Chagall (Galerie Hodebert). Nouvelle Revue Française 24:253-5 F 1 1925.

104 LICHTENSTEIN, ISAAC. Marc Chagall. 15p plus 15 plates Paris, "Le Triangle," 1927. (Jewish artists monographs)
Yiddish text.

* 105 LILIENFELD GALLERIES, NEW YORK. Marc Chagall. 3p 1939.
Exhibition catalog listing 15 works.

* 106 ———Marc Chagall. 3p 1938.
Exhibition catalog listing 16 works.

107 LOZOWICK, LOUIS. Marc Chagall. il Jewish Survey 1no8:16-17 Ja 1942.

108 ———Marc Chagall. il Menorah Journal 10:343-6 Ag-S 1924.

* 109 ———Chagall's "Circus." il Theatre Arts Monthly 13no8:593-601 Ag 1929.

110 LUKOMSKY, G. K. Exhibition of the works of Chagall. Nakanune (Berlin) Ja 9 1923.
Russian text. Exhibition, Galerie Lutz, Berlin.

† 111 LUZZATTO, GUIDO LODOVICO. Chagall. 9p Citta di Castello, 1930.

112 ———Note sur Chagall à l'occasion de l'exposition Chagall à la Kunsthalle de Bâle. Revue Juive de Genève 2no2:81-3 N 1933.
Appended is a note addressed to Chagall by the Museum of Tel Aviv expressing regret over the destruction of one of Chagall's paintings by the Nazis.

113 ———[Review of] Marc Chagall: *Ma vie.* Il Convegno (Milan) D 25 1932.

114 MAI, GALERIE, PARIS. Marc Chagall. 3p il 1940.
Exhibition catalog listing 30 works.

MANUEL, ROLAND. See 59.

* 115 MARC CHAGALL. 19p il Berlin, Verlag Der Sturm, 1923. (Sturm-Bilderbuch I)
Includes poem by Blaise Cendrars (see bibl. 17).

* 115a MARC CHAGALL. il Salient (New York) no3:10-13 D 1944.

* 116 MARC CHAGALL. 152p il Anvers, Éditions Sélection, 1929. (Sélection: chronique de la vie artistique. 6)
Includes bibliography, essays by André de Ridder, Waldemar George, Maurice Raynal, Jacques Maritain, Pierre Courthion, Georges Charensol, Joseph Delteil, Ambroise Vollard (reprinted from bibl. 185), Karl With, Abraham Efross, Chagall (reprinted from bibl. 5) and poems by Guillaume Apollinaire, Blaise Cendrars, André Salmon and Paul Fierens.

* 117 MARC CHAGALL'S DESIGNS FOR ALEKO AND THE FIREBIRD. il (some col) Dance Index 4no11:185-204 1945.
"The artist and the ballet" by George Amberg, p188, 204.

* 118 MARITAIN, JACQUES. Art and poetry. p17-21 New York, Philosophical Library, 1943.
Text dated 1929; 1934. Published, in part, accompanied by illustrations, under title:
* *Eaux-fortes de Chagall pour la Bible* in Cahiers d'Art 9no4:84-92 1934.

———See also 116.

* 119 MARITAIN, RAÏSSA. Marc Chagall. 50p plus 7 plates New York, Éditions de la Maison Française, 1943.
Includes poem; also "Une interview de Chagall" reprinted from bibl. 143.

120 MARLIER, GEORGES. Chagall et nous. il Nation Belge (Brussels) F 1 1938.
Occasioned by exhibition of Chagall's work at Palais des Beaux-Arts, Brussels.

* 121 MATISSE, PIERRE, GALLERY, NEW YORK. Chagall, paintings—gouaches. folder [1943]
Exhibition catalog listing 21 works.

* 122 ———Marc Chagall. 2p il [1944]
Exhibition catalog listing 25 works.

* 122a ———Marc Chagall, paintings, gouaches. 3p 1942.
Exhibition catalog listing 16 works.

* 123 ———Paintings, 1945-1946: Marc Chagall. folder il 1946.
Exhibition catalog listing 21 works.

* 124 ———Retrospective exhibition of paintings and gouaches from 1910 to 1941: Marc Chagall. 3p il 1941.
Exhibition catalog listing 21 works.

125 MIL, JOS. Marc Chagall en Palestine. Appui Français (Paris) O 1 1931.
Interview with Chagall. Reprinted from Univers Israelite.

* 126 MILLER, HENRY. Marc Chagall. *In* the author's Semblance of a devoted past. p23 Berkeley, Bern Porter, 1944.

127 NAVON, ARYEH & GOLDBERG, LEAH, ed. The Jewish village in the paintings of Marc Chagall. 8p plus 24 plates (1 col) Tel Aviv, "Sifriat Poalim" Worker's Book-Guild (Hashomer Hatzair), 1943.
Hebrew text.

128 NEW ART CIRCLE, NEW YORK. Marc Chagall: flowers and dreams. folder 1936.
Exhibition catalog.

* 129 NEW YORK. MUSEUM OF MODERN ART. Fantastic art, dada, surrealism, ed. by Alfred H. Barr, Jr. p114-16,259 il 1936.

* 130 ———Modern painters and sculptors as illustrators, ed. by Monroe Wheeler. p18, 59, 99 il 1936.

* 131 ———20th century portraits, by Monroe Wheeler. p22,64-5,135 il 1942.

132 OSBORN, MAX. L'art fantastique de Chagall. De Telegraaf (Amsterdam) Mr 5 1940.

133 ———100 Fabeln von Marc Chagall. Vossische Zeitung (Berlin) Ap 12 1930.
Exhibition, Galerie Flechtheim, Berlin.

134 ———Marc Chagall. il (some col) Zhar-Ptitsa (Berlin) no11:13-21 1923.

* 135 PAULDING, C. G. Marc Chagall. il Liturgical Arts 11no3:66-7 My 1943.

* 136 PAYRO, JULIO E. Pintura moderna. p204-6 il Buenos Aires, Editorial Poseidon, 1942.

* 137 POGGIOLI, RENATO. Marc Chagall. il Decision 3no1-2:63-5 Ja-F 1942.

138 POPOV, N. N. Experiment in studying works of art from the point of view of their psychophysical constitution: Marc Chagall. Journal of Neuropathology and Psychiatry (Moscow) 22no3-4:499-510 1929.
Russian text.

139 LE PORTIQUE, GALERIE, PARIS. Chagall: gouaches et illustrations. 4p il 1928.
Exhibition catalog with preface by Coquiot extracted from bibl. 48.

140 ———20 tableaux récents de Marc Chagall et quelques dessins de jeunesse inédits. 2p 1931.
Exhibition catalog.

141 PREVANNE, A. Le folklore dans l'art de Marc Chagall. il Monde (Paris) 3no113:8 Ag 2 1930.
In part, an interview with Chagall.

142 RAVEL, MARCEL. L'exposition Chagall à la Galerie Mai. il Prométhée 20no9-10:298-9 D 1939/Ja 1940.

* 143 RAYNAL, MAURICE. Anthologie de la peinture en France de 1906 à nos jours. p93-8 il Paris, Éditions Montaigne, 1927.
Includes statements by Chagall. Reprinted, in part, in bibl. 119. Translated into English in the author's Modern French painters. p55-8 il New York, Brentano's, 1928.

———See also 116.

* 144 REINHARDT GALLERIES, NEW YORK. Marc Chagall exhibition. 9p il por 1926.
Exhibition catalog listing 100 works. Introduction by Christian Brinton.

145 REY, ROBERT. A propos de l'exposition Marc Chagall. Europe Nouvelle (Paris) 8no360:54 Ja 10 1925.
Exhibition, Galerie Barbazanges-Hodebert, Paris.

146 RIDDER, ANDRÉ DE. Chagall. il Beaux Arts (Brussels) D 22 1933.
Occasioned by Chagall exhibition in Basel. Reprinted with slight changes from Le Démocrate (Basel) N 6 1933.

147 ———La Fontaine vu par Chagall. Variétés (Brussels) 2no10:735-6 F 15 1930.

149 ———Marc Chagall. Sélection (Antwerp) ns 3e année 2:103-6 Ap 1924.
Exhibition, Galerie Le Centaure, Paris.

———See also 116

150 ROGER-MARX, CLAUDE. Une gouache de Chagall. il Europe Nouvelle (Paris) 11no562: 1569 N 17 1928.

151 SALMON, ANDRÉ. Chagall. il Art Vivant 1no22:1-3 N 15 1925.
Includes statements by Chagall quoted from bibl.65.

* 152 ———Chagall. 21p plus 44 plates. Paris, Éditions des Chroniques du Jour, 1928.

153 ———Chagall illustrateur. Paris Matinal Jy 4 1927.
Criticism inspired by Chagall's illustrations for Coquiot's *Suite Provinciale*.

154 ———Le salon. Montjoie (Paris) 2no3:21-8 Mr 1914.
"Chagall," p23.

———See also 29.

155 SCHATZ, BEZALEL. Marc Chagall. il Jewish Layman (Cincinnati) 16no5:6-8 Ja 1942.

156 SCHEFFLER, KARL. Marc Chagall. il Kunst und Künstler 21:39-47 N 1922.

157 SCHMIDT, GEORG. Le merveilleux dans l'art de Marc Chagall. il Labyrinthe (Geneva) 1no3:9 D 15 1944.

158 SCHMITZ, MARCEL. Les Fables de La Fontaine. Traduites par Chagall. Avenir du Luxembourg (Arlon) Mr 17 1930.

159 SCHWOB, J. ALFRED. Un tableau de Chagall. Chalom (Paris) 14no87:7-9 Ja 1935.

* 160 SCHWOB, RENÉ. Chagall et l'âme juive. 135p il Paris, Corrêa, 1931.

161 ———Chagall, peintre juif. il Amour de l'Art 9:305-9 Ag 1928.
Text dated 1924.

* 162 ———Les Fables de La Fontaine par Chagall. il Cahiers d'Art 3no4:167-9 1928.

———See also 167.

SÉLECTION. Number devoted to Marc Chagall. See 116.

† 163 SEROUYA, HENRI. Art et philosophie. Tour de Babel no1:35-45 N 1 1925.

164 ———Marc Chagall. il por Illustration Juive (Alexandria, Egypt) 2no5:17-19 Mr 1930.

165 SOUPAULT, PHILIPPE. Les eaux fortes de Marc Chagall. il Amour de l'Art 7:180-4 My 1926.
* Reprinted in Der Querschnitt 6:839-43 N 1926.

166 ———Marc Chagall. il Feuilles Libres 6no37:55-7 S-O 1924.
12 drawings by Chagall are reproduced in the issue.

167 SPIRE, ANDRÉ. Marc Chagall. Appui Français (Paris) Jy-Ag 1932.
Remarks on Chagall's *Ma Vie* and on Chagall's critics, Salmon, Guenne and Schwob. A letter by Schwob based on this article together with Spire's answer to it is published in Appui Français S 1932. Further response by Spire appears in the O 1932 number.

* 168 SWEENEY, JAMES JOHNSON. An interview with Marc Chagall. Partisan Review 11no1:88-93 Winter 1944.
* Reprinted, in part, in Goldwater, Robert & Treves, Marco. Artists on art. p432-4 il New York, Pantheon Books, 1945.

* 169 SYLVÈRE, JEAN. Portraits d'artistes . . . Chagall. Cahiers d'Art 4no5:232 1929.

170 SZECSI, LADISLAS. Marc Chagall. il Kunst and Künstler 31:324-9 S 1932.
Includes statements by Chagall.

171 SZITTYA, EMIL. Chagall: eine Diskussion gegen seine Freunde. il Der Querschnitt 2:205-7 Weihnachtsheft 1922.

† 172 ———Malerschicksale. Hamburg, 1925.
Includes essay on Chagall.

* 173 TÉRIADE, E. Documentaire sur la jeune peinture. il Cahiers d'Art 5no2:71,75 1930.

* 174 ———Marc Chagall. il Cahiers d'Art 1no6:122-7 1926.

TREVES, MARCO. See 168.

175 TUGENDHOLD, Ia. Marc Chagall. il Apollon (Petrograd) no2:11-20 1916.
Russian text.

———See also 61.

* 176 TZARA, TRISTAN. Marc Chagall. il Cahiers d'Art 14no5-10:148-9 1939.
Text dated 1921.

* 177 UHDE, WILHELM. Picasso et la tradition française. p83-4 il Paris, Éditions des Quatre Chemins, 1928.

* 178 UMANSKY, KONSTANTIN. Neue Kunst in Russland, 1914-1919. p18-19,27 il Potsdam, G. Kiepenheuer; München, H. Goltz, 1920.

179 VANDERPYL, FRITZ R. Peintres de mon époque. p181-8 Paris, Stock, 1931.

* 180 VENTURI, LIONELLO. Chagall chez Pierre Matisse. Spectateur des Arts (Paris) no1:30-1 D 1944.

* 181 ———Marc Chagall. 55p plus 64 plates. New York, Pierre Matisse Editions, 1945.
Includes bibliography.

* 182 ———Painting and painters. p230-2 il New York, Scribner's, 1945.

* 183 VIGEVENO, JAMES, GALLERIES, LOS ANGELES. Marc Chagall. 7p il 1945.
Exhibition catalog listing 29 works.

184 VINCENT, LÉANDRE. Art et miracle. Paris Journal Jy 3 1924.
Criticism of the artist's *Double Portrait* exhibited at the Salon des Tuileries, Paris.

185 VOLLARD, AMBROISE. De La Fontaine à Chagall. il L'Intransigeant (Paris) Ja 8, 14 1929.
Reprinted in part (text of Ja 14) in Der
* Querschnitt 10hft3:183-4 Mr 1930, in Frankfurter Zeitung Mr 29 1930, in bibl. 33 and in bibl. 116.

* 186 ———Recollections of a picture dealer. p260-1 il Boston, Little, Brown, 1936.
Also published in French under title: Souvenirs d'un marchand de tableaux. Paris, Michel, 1937.

WALDEN, HERWARTH, ed. See 17.

187 WARNOD, ANDRÉ. Le réalisme et la fantaisie dans l'oeuvre de Marc Chagall. il Comoedia (Paris) D 15 1924.
Exhibition, Galerie Barbazanges-Hodebert, Paris.

188 WATT, ALEXANDER. Notes from Paris. Apollo 23no134:105-8 F 1936.
Exhibition, *Peintres Instinctifs* (bibl.29).

189 WEIDLE, WLADIMIR. Notes on Chagall. il Chisla (Paris) 9:176-8 1933.
Russian text.

190 ———Notes sur Chagall. il Le Point (Colmar) 2no5:208-12 N 1937.

* 190a WERNER, ALFRED. Marc Chagall, painter of love. il por Free World 11no4:42-6 Ap 1946.

WESTHEIM, PAUL, ed. See 5.

WHEELER, MONROE. See 130, 131.

* 191 WILENSKI, REGINALD HOWARD. Modern French painters. passim New York, Reynal & Hitchcock, 1940.

———See also 99.

* 192 WILLRICH, WOLFGANG. Säuberung des Kunsttempels: eine kunstpolitische Kampfschrift zur Gesundung deutscher Kunst im Geiste nordischer Art. p87-8 München, J. F. Lehmann, 1937.

* 193 WITH, KARL. Marc Chagall. 16p plus 33 plates (1 col) Leipzig, Klinkhardt & Biermann, 1923. (Junge Kunst, Bd 35)
* Also published in Der Cicerone 15no16:
* 726-39 Ag 1923 and in Jahrbuch der Jungen Kunst 1923:160-73.

———See also 116.

194 ZEMACH, S. Chagall. il por Moznayim (Tel Aviv) 2no45:1-2 Mr 1931.
Hebrew text.

* 195 ZERVOS, CHRISTIAN. De la nécessité d'une importante exposition des peintures de Chagall. il Cahiers d'Art 14no5-10:146-7 1939.

* 196 ———Les Fables de La Fontaine. Cahiers d'Art 5no1:52-3 1930.
Exhibition, Galerie Bernheim, Paris.

* 197 ———Histoire de l'art contemporain. p341-50 il Paris, Éditions "Cahiers d'Art," 1938.

* 198 ———Marc Chagall. il (1 col) Art d'Aujourd'hui Winter 1924:25-30, plates 24-30.

199 ———Marc Chagall. il Drawing and Design 4no19:7-14, 19 Ja 1928.

* 200 ———Note sur une exposition d'oeuvres récentes de Chagall. il Cahiers d'Art 6no7-8: 348-9 1931.
Exhibition, Galerie Le Portique, Paris.

APPENDIX

Translations of poems on pages 18 and 29-30.

ROTSOGE

To the painter Chagall

Your scarlet face your biplane convertible into hydroplane
Your round house where a smoked herring swims
I must have a key to eyelids
It's a good thing we have seen Mr. Panado
And we are easy on that score
What do you want my old pal M.D.
90 or 324 a man in the air a calf who gazes out of the belly of its mother
I looked a long while along the roads
So many eyes are closed at the roadside
The wind sets the willow groves weeping
Open open open open open
Look but look now
The old man is bathing his feet in the basin
Una volta ho inteso say Ach du lieber Gott
And I began to cry reminiscing over our childhoods
And you show me a dreadful purple
This little painting where there is a cart which reminded me of the day
A day made out of pieces of mauves yellows blues greens and reds
When I left for the country with a charming chimney holding its bitch in leash
I had a reed pipe which I would not have traded for a French Marshal's baton
There aren't any more of them I haven't my little reed pipe any more
The chimney smokes far away from me Russian cigarettes
Its bitch barks against the lilacs
And the vigil lamp is burned out
On the dress petals have fallen
Two gold rings near some sandals
Kindle in the sun
While your hair is like the trolley cable
Across Europe arrayed in little many-colored fires.

Spring, 1914

GUILLAUME APOLLINAIRE

From ENFANCE

In the wood there is a bird, his song stops you and makes you blush.

There is a clock that does not strike.

There is a pit with a nest of white creatures.

There is a cathedral that goes down and a lake that rises.

There is a little cart left behind in the coppice or that runs down the path, all ribbony.

There is a company of little actors in costume, just barely seen on the road through the skirt of the wood.

There is at last, when you are hungry and thirsty, someone who chases you away.

ARTHUR RIMBAUD

Seventeen thousand and five hundred copies of this book have been printed in May 1946 for the Trustees of the Museum of Modern Art by the Plantin Press, New York. The color inserts were printed by William E. Rudge's Sons, New York.

ChAg
ALL